LOST BALTIMORE

Acknowledgments

The authors wish to thank David Salmo and Frank Hopkinson of Anova Books for their help with this book; Maryland Historical Society; Library of Congress; Enoch Pratt Library; the *Baltimore Sun*; Daniel Van Allen; and Baltimore Heritage.

Picture credits

All images are courtesy of Library of Congress, except for the following:

Courtesy of the authors: 8, 9 (left), 10, 12 (right), 13, 28, 32–33, 39 (top), 41 (right), 42–43, 46 (top), 47, 48–51, 54–55, 71, 85 (left), 88–89, 102 (left), 104 (left), 105 (bottom right), 106 (left), 107, 109, 112, 125–126, 140–143.

Anova Image Library: 17, 18, 23, 27, 39 (bottom), 40, 41 (left), 46 (bottom), 53, 56 (left), 61 (right), 70, 80–81, 91, 96–98, 99 (left), 100–101, 123–124, 137, 139.

Maryland Historical Society: 14, 15 (right), 31, 38, 82, 108, 127.

Corbis: 37 (top), 93, 110–111, 116.

Getty Images: 52 (right), 58, 83, 113, 117.

Hughes Company Glass Negatives Collection, University of Maryland, Baltimore County: 102 (right), 104 (right), 105 (left and top right).

Robin L.J.: 136 (right).

Patrick Semansky: 138.

Endpapers

Front: Bird's-eye view of Baltimore, 1880.
Back: View of Baltimore from Federal Hill, 1847.

First published in the United Kingdom in 2013 by
PAVILION BOOKS
10 Southcombe Street, London W14 0RA
An imprint of Anova Books Company Ltd

© Anova Books, 2013

ISBN: 978-1-90910-843-1

A CIP catalogue record for this book is available from the British Library.

10 9 8 7 6 5 4 3 2

Repro by Rival Colour Ltd, UK
Printed by 1010 Printing International Ltd, China

www.anovabooks.com

LOST BALTIMORE

Gregory J. Alexander &
Paul Kelsey Williams

PAVILION

LOST IN THE...

INTRODUCTION

Baltimore, like most urban metropolitan cities, has undergone dramatic changes in its landscape—its physical makeup through the erection and demolition of notable buildings in and around its city core, as well as changes to the population demographics and changes dictated by societal trends.

Baltimore's population increased significantly beginning in the 1840s and 1850s, as the city grew to be the second-largest city in the country. Population growth continued over the next century, as Baltimore remained as the seventh or eighth biggest city in the United States, and in the 1950s and 1960s, Baltimore had just shy of one million residents. However, after the riots of the 1960s and the turbulent times of the 1970s, Baltimore's population plummeted as more and more city dwellers headed to the suburbs for better schools, a quieter lifestyle, and more green space. In recent years, the city's population has held steady with just over 600,000 residents calling Baltimore home.

Baltimore has also lost its share of iconic buildings along the way. The grand estates of northern Baltimore are long gone, as rows and rows of brick homes have replaced the bucolic environment of the 19th century. However, the greatest change to the physical landscape was caused by the devastating Great Baltimore Fire of 1904. The fire that erupted on the morning of February 7, 1904, destroyed more than 1,500 buildings that made up the 140-acre central business core in just over 48 hours. It caused an estimated $150 million in damage in 1904, which is equivalent to approximately $3.8 billion today.

Some of the most noteworthy buildings lost in the fire include the Baltimore & Ohio Railroad headquarters, the Sun Iron Building, and the News American Building. However, Baltimore showed its resolve shortly after the fire as a string of buildings were constructed downtown immediately thereafter as a show of resilience.

In addition to changes in the physical makeup of the city, this book also chronicles many of the societal changes over the years. Baltimore's dominance as a manufacturing, shipping, and ship-building capital in the early 20th century are illustrated, as well as changes dictated by evolving lifestyles, such as the elimination of streetcars and lessening of somewhat quirky behaviors, such as scrubbing the marble front steps of your home on a weekly basis. Baltimore has also lost some of its entertainment outlets such as Riverview Park, Electric Park, public beaches, and many public swimming pools. Not all changes are negative, of course—the elimination of the inadequate Baltimore Municipal Airport in favor of the more sophisticated Baltimore-Washington International Thurgood Marshall Airport has aided the city's growth.

In this book, we also highlight those buildings that remain, although in much different forms. Lexington Market has burned several times, but each time, it comes back bigger and better than before; the famed Bromo-Seltzer Tower remains an iconic building downtown, even though the adjacent factory and whimsical spinning bottle are long gone.

Notable moments in history that have significantly shaped Baltimore are also included, most importantly the heartbreaking loss of the beloved Baltimore Colts in 1984, as well as the abrupt vanishing of the "Poe Toaster" in honor of Edgar Allen Poe, the famed writer who died in Baltimore.

Of course, there is too much to cover in Baltimore's history for one book, so there are many omissions that space or inadequate photographic resources dictated. Thankfully, there are some areas that could not be included because they have witnessed a comeback, such as the beloved painted screens in East Baltimore that continue on today, thanks to a dedicated group of artists.

Gregory J. Alexander & Paul Kelsey Williams

RIGHT *The Tower Building on East Baltimore Street (see page 122.)*

First Presbyterian Church **DEMOLISHED 1860**

The First Presbyterian Church (now called First and Franklin Presbyterian Church after the two congregations merged in 1973) is now located in the Mount Vernon in a beautiful Gothic church. However, this building is actually the church's fourth home in Baltimore.

According to First Presbyterian Church, the church was founded in 1761 by several Scotch-Irish families who came to Baltimore from rural Pennsylvania to escape the French and Indian War. These parishioners were known as "dissenters" because they opposed the Church of England as the established state church. They also supported the American Revolution, and advocated for the separation of church and state.

First Presbyterian Church's first minister was Reverend Patrick Allison, who was born in Pennsylvania in 1740. After graduating from the University of Pennsylvania, he began studying theology, and eventually was licensed to preach by the Second Presbytery of Philadelphia. In 1763, he moved to Baltimore, and became the founding minister of Baltimore's first Presbyterian church, to

be aptly named, First Presbyterian Church. In addition to his notoriety as the founding chaplain of First Presbyterian Church, Reverend Allison also represented the Presbytery of Baltimore at the first meeting of the General Assembly in Philadelphia in 1789, was Chaplain to the Continental Congress, and was a close friend of George Washington. He remained as pastor of First Presbyterian until his death in 1802.

First Presbyterian Church held services in private homes in the beginning, but in 1763, upon arrival of Revered Allison, services were then held in a log church. A brick church was built two years later, and beginning in 1790, a large two-steeple church was constructed to accommodate the growing congregation, and it was referred to as one of the largest and most magnificent church buildings in the whole land. The large church at East Fayette Street and Guilford Avenue (called North Street during this time) was completed in 1795 and would serve as the church's home until 1859. It featured four enormous Roman Doric stone columns and cost approximately $20,000 to

construct. The large chapel would seat 1,000 parishioners, which included Mayor James Calhoun. John Dalrymple was the architect of the church with James Mosher hired as the bricklayer.

The Board of Foreign Missions of the Presbyterian General Assembly met at First Presbyterian Church in Baltimore in 1837, and later missionaries were sent to Mexico, Japan, India, Brazil, China, and other countries to spread the teachings of the Presbyterian Church.

According to the First Presbyterian Church, the increasingly congested and commercial environs of the neighborhood caused the church to look for an alternate location. The church looked slightly north to the scenic neighborhood of Mount Vernon and chose the location of Park Avenue and Madison Street for its fourth church location.

A September 19, 1859 article in the *Baltimore Sun* detailed the last service held on East Fayette Street:

The closing services in the old First Presbyterian Church, at the corner of Fayette and North Sts., were held yesterday, and were of a very impressive and interesting character. The church property has been sold, and the services of yesterday were the farewell to a church building, the oldest in the city and hallowed by sacred remembrances. At an early hour, the building was thronged in every part, and so great was the desire of the people to be present at the occasion that it was found necessary to fill all the isles with seats.

While the new Mount Vernon church was being finalized in its construction, services were held in the courthouse. The new church was built at Madison Street and Park Avenue and remains today. Its striking Gothic architecture and triple-vaulted ceiling inside were designed by architect Nathan Starkweather, and a 273-foot-tall steeple was later added, the tallest in Baltimore even today. The church was placed on the National Register of Historic Places in 1973.

First Presbyterian's former location on East Fayette, however, was razed in 1860 to build a courthouse, which was later demolished to make way for a new post office.

ABOVE *First Presbyterian Church's current building under construction at Madison Street and Park Avenue.*

RIGHT *The East Fayette Street church held services from 1795 to 1859.*

OPPOSITE PAGE *A view of Mount Vernon from the top of First Presbyterian Church's current location.*

Fort Federal Hill Barracks GONE 1880

Federal Hill provides some of the most scenic views of Baltimore. The large grass hill is a popular spot for tourists to climb for unobstructed views of Baltimore's Harbor. Due to its height and central location, Federal Hill was also once occupied by Union troops and transformed into a military stronghold flanked by barracks, cannons, tents, and other militaria.

Federal Hill was originally called "John Smith's Hill" after Captain John Smith, the English explorer who wrote about the hill during his journeys along the Chesapeake Bay from Jamestown, Virginia. The present name, Federal Hill, derives from a celebration in 1788 when Baltimore residents paraded through the streets to commemorate the State of Maryland's ratification of the United States Constitution. A 15-foot model of a ship was constructed and named the "Federalist." The ship was wheeled through the streets, organized by Revolutionary War hero Joshua Barney, and eventually was set sail in the Inner Harbor. The name "John Smith's Hill" was then changed to Federal Hill in honor of the "Federalist."

Federal Hill was used as a lookout station during the Battle of Baltimore in 1814, in anticipation of a British invasion of the city. However, the British defeat at nearby Fort McHenry prevented such attack.

Federal Hill was almost demolished in 1838 when a plan was proposed to raze the hill, fill the basin, and extend adjacent thoroughfares. Thankfully, the plan was not realized, mostly for financial reasons.

However, Federal Hill's most notable historic event was the Civil War. After the Southern secession and bombardment at Fort Sumter, South Carolina, President Abraham Lincoln called for troops to be transported from the states to Washington, D.C., to protect the nation's capital. In route to Washington, D.C., the troops would pass through Baltimore via train. Many Baltimoreans were sympathetic to the southern states' right to succeed from the Union, and on April 1861, as the 6th Massachusetts Infantry was changing trains from the President Street Station to the Camden Station (train cars had to be disconnected and pulled by horse down Pratt Street to the Camden Station), a mob forced the cars to return to the President Street Station. The 6th Massachusetts Infantry then marched down Pratt Street, citizens began throwing stones, and gunfire shot out. The "Pratt Street Riots" were the first casualties of the Civil War, as 12 people were killed.

In response, the Governor and Mayor called out the militia, and soon thereafter, the 6th Massachusetts Infantry constructed earthworks on Federal Hill. Cannons, gun encampments, fortifications, and tents were installed, creating "Fort Federal Hill." It's been reported that the strongest cannon was pointed at the Maryland Club in Mount Vernon, known as a gathering place for Confederate sympathizers. By 1862, barracks had been built for 1,000 men at Fort Federal Hill, a wall was built around the Fort, and an 80-foot well was dug to supply fresh water access for the Union troops.

Further, those sympathetic to the Southern cause were arrested and imprisoned at nearby Fort McHenry. Union troops would remain at Fort Federal Hill until after the end of the Civil War. In 1880, the City of Baltimore purchased Federal Hill and converted it into a public park. With the exception of the cannons, there are little remains left of the Fort.

Another notable element missing from Federal Hill today is the maritime observation tower. Several versions of the tower have existed with the first being constructed around 1797 when Captain David Porter established a marine observatory and signal tower. In the signal tower was a watchman who upon seeing a ship would unfurl a flag to alert the Maritime Exchange. In 1885, the old observatory was razed, and in 1887, an ornate new tower in a Victorian gingerbread design was erected, complete with an ice cream parlor on the lower level. However, the new tower was unstable from its inception and was rarely used due to advancements in communications technology. In 1902, a violent storm caused the tower to collapse and was never replaced.

LEFT *Due to Federal Hill's waterfront location, the government feared an attack during the War of 1812.*

RIGHT *An 1862 lithograph showing Fort Federal Hill from the east, interior, south, and west.*

INTERIOR.

FROM THE EAST.

FROM THE SOUTH.

Bolton RAZED 1901

Bolton Hill is one of Baltimore's most picturesque neighborhoods with its rich history, abundant green space, and tony residences. The neighborhood's origin can be traced back to three vast estates—Bolton, Rose Hill, and Mount Royal. William Gibson owned Rose Hill, Solomon Birkhead owned Mount Royal, while George Grundy owned Bolton. The rural area was one of the highest points in the city, offering respite from the heat experienced downtown.

Grundy named his estate after his English birthplace, Bolton-le-Moors. Grundy, born in 1755, married Mary Carr, and the couple had five children. Grundy, a successful merchant in Baltimore, acquired 30 acres in 1793 and immediately began construction on his Bolton estate.

Bolton was an enormous 65-foot-by-37-foot, two-story, brick home with a central tower and a columned front portico. The Federal style home also featured a two-story bay window, engaged columns at each corner, hipped roof, and wide entrance hall. In its time, its facade was considered one of the most beautiful in all of Baltimore. Also on the large property were a barn, two coach houses, smokehouse, and an ice house.

The Bolton estate was also notable for its exquisite gardens and orchards of peach, apple, and cherry trees. Grundy was so enamored with his gardens that he built a two-story residence for the gardener. The gardens were tremendous—the plantings were three times the width of the house and included a kitchen garden and extensive gravel paths for exploring the various plants and trees.

Unfortunately, Grundy suffered enormous financial setbacks and eventually lost Bolton. He died in Baltimore in 1825 at the age of 70. Bolton was subsequently sold to William Wallace Spence. In 1901, Bolton was demolished to make way for the Fifth Regiment Armory, which would host the 1912 Democratic National Convention, where Woodrow Wilson was nominated for president.

Bolton Hill, which was called Mount Royal until the 1950s, experienced major development in the mid- to late 1800s. Rows and rows of brick homes were constructed, many in the Queen Anne style, along with major estates and historic churches and synagogues, followed by large apartment buildings. One of the most interesting elements of Bolton Hill's design is that unlike many Baltimore neighborhoods, which were designed in a north-south pattern of streets, Bolton Hill is a series of diagonal streets and planned garden squares. Surveyor Thomas Poppleton is credited with this unique neighborhood plan. In addition to the planned gardens, residents also benefit from close proximity to the 500-acre Druid Hill Park.

The original big three estate owners—William Gibson, Solomon Birkhead, and George Grundy—were just a few of the prominent citizens to call Bolton Hill home. In the late 1800s, many professors at Johns Hopkins University lived here, as well as the school's first president, Daniel Coit Gilman. The neighborhood's proximity to Johns Hopkins as well as the Maryland Institute College of Art draws college students and professors even today.

Many famous cultural figures have also lived in Bolton Hill, including the Cone sisters, who started the Baltimore Museum of Art, and writers Scott and Zelda Fitzgerald. The Bolton Hill historic district—bounded by North Avenue, Eutaw Place and Pennsylvania Railroad tracks—was listed on the National Register of Historic Places in 1971.

ABOVE *George Grundy acquired 30 acres of land for the construction of the Bolton estate.*

RIGHT *The Federal style facade of the Bolton mansion was considered one of the most beautiful in Baltimore.*

LEFT *Bolton was demolished in 1901 for the construction of the Fifth Regiment Armory, which remains today.*

Merchants' Exchange RAZED 1901

BENJAMIN HENRY LATROBE

The Merchants' Exchange building was just one of the many prominent buildings designed by Benjamin Henry Latrobe, known as the "Father of American Architecture." Born in England and educated in Europe, Latrobe thrived at an early age in the field of architecture. However, he also suffered hardship when his wife died in 1793 while giving birth to the couple's third child. Latrobe struggled professionally, too, and soon set sail for the United States with his children, landing in Virginia in 1796. While in Virginia, he designed a prison in Richmond before moving to Philadelphia and then Washington, D.C., Latrobe's work in Philadelphia had caught the attention of President Thomas Jefferson, who hired him to design the U.S. Capitol, a project that would take over 10 years to complete. He is also well known as the architect of the Basilica of the Assumption of the Blessed Virgin Mary, also known as the Baltimore Basilica and America's First Basilica. In 1821, while working on a waterworks system in New Orleans, Latrobe contracted yellow fever and died. His sons, John and Benjamin, however, stayed in Baltimore, and became an architect and engineer respectively.

Baltimore's role as a maritime power in the 19th and 20th centuries is well documented. Its strategic location, proximity to the Chesapeake Bay, access to the most sophisticated railroad system in the United States, and the ability to transport goods easily either north to Philadelphia and New York City or west to Chicago all contributed to Baltimore's importance in the maritime community.

And as foreign trade increased, Baltimore continued to boast a vital commercial port. In 1789, the U.S. Congress established the United States Customs Service and determined that Baltimore would serve as one of the collection districts. To house Baltimore's custom house, the Merchants' Exchange Building was constructed beginning in 1815 at the intersection of Gay and Water Streets downtown.

Maximilian Godefroy and renowned architect Benjamin Henry Latrobe (see sidebar) were hired as architects for the Merchants' Exchange building. Godefroy had designed other prominent buildings in Baltimore, including the Battle Monument, St. Mary's Seminary Chapel, and the Unitarian Church. However, while working on the Merchants' Exchange building, Godefroy and Latrobe had a major falling out. It was understood that Latrobe would contribute the overall design, while Godefroy was to execute the drawings and supervise construction. However, Godefroy changed Latrobe's plans to incorporate his own ideas. Latrobe always gave Godefroy credit for the front of the building, but the two parted ways. Godefroy contended that Latrobe was the reason that he was unable to obtain future commissions in Baltimore, and he left Baltimore in 1819 to return to England to tend to his daughter who was dying of yellow fever.

The Merchants' Exchange building was designed in a Greco-Roman design with a dramatic dome that was an architectural highlight of downtown Baltimore at the time. The dome also had promenades, offering picturesque views of the Baltimore waterfront. In addition to the customs house, the Merchants' Exchange building also contained a stock exchange, bank, hotel, post office, and a venue for special events.

Shortly after completion, General Marquis de Lafayette visited in 1824. However, the most important event to take place at the Merchants' Exchange building occurred on April 21, 1865, when the body of President Abraham Lincoln was laid in state. President Lincoln, who had been assassinated the week prior and died in the early morning hours of April 15, was transported by a train of dark-garlanded cars from Washington, D.C., to Baltimore's Camden Station. His coffin was then taken to the Merchants' Exchange Building to lie in state. The somber event included a public viewing, attended by approximately 10,000 people in three hours. After the viewing, his coffin was taken by train to Harrisburg, Pennsylvania.

In 1901, the Merchants' Exchange building was razed, and a new custom house was built on the same site. However, the 1904 Great Baltimore Fire severely damaged the new building. Much of the building had to be rebuilt, but by 1907, the Beaux-Arts designed building was complete.

OPPOSITE PAGE AND BELOW *The Merchants' Exchange being razed in 1901. Abraham Lincoln lay in state here after his assassination in 1865.*

Baltimore & Ohio Headquarters BURNED 1904

Baltimoreans love their railroad, and for good reason. Perhaps no other American city has been shaped by the railroad as much as Charm City. Even today, visitors have two railroad museums in town—one in Baltimore's West Side and one in nearby Ellicott City, both dedicated to the famed Baltimore & Ohio (B&O) Railroad. In addition to the various train stations in Baltimore, the city was also home to the Baltimore & Ohio headquarters.

The Baltimore and Ohio Rail Road Company was America's first common carrier, chartered in 1827 by a group of Baltimore businessmen to ensure traffic would not be lost to the proposed Chesapeake & Ohio Canal. By 1835, the B&O extended to Washington, and the U.S. Postal Service began utilizing the B&O by 1838. The B&O then stretched into western Maryland, Virginia and what is now West Virginia by the 1850s. During the Civil War, the B&O moved Union troops and supplies, despite Confederate attacks. In the late 1860s, the railroad reached Ohio, then Chicago by 1874, and St. Louis followed with the acquisition of the Marietta & Cincinnati Railroad, and the Ohio & Mississippi Railroad.

With this massive growth, the B&O needed a new headquarters building.

The B&O's new headquarters building was the vision of John Work Garrett, who served as president of the B&O from 1858 until his death in 1884. His tenure at the B&O was highlighted by western expansion to Chicago and his support of the Union cause during the Civil War. The grand Second Empire building with unique awnings to help block out the sun was located on the northwest corner of Baltimore and Calvert Streets. The location previously was the home to the Baltimore Museum, which was destroyed by fire in 1872. Ironically, the B&O building would suffer the same fate. The B&O purchased the land and entrusted E. Francis Baldwin, its head architect, with its design (see sidebar) in 1882.

Baldwin first envisioned a five-story building, but that was expanded to seven stories to provide the space the railroad company needed. Two additional stories were added in 1888.

Tragically, the B&O headquarters building was severely damaged in the 1904 Baltimore Fire. The building was razed and the site was filled by the Emerson Hotel, a 17-story hotel, which opened in 1911, closed in 1969, and was demolished in 1971. Meanwhile, the B&O moved its headquarters to a new building on North Charles Street.

The new B&O headquarters featured many of the opulent features of its previous home. Constructed in 1906, the 13-story, steel-framed building was designed by the architectural firm of Parker & Thomas and featured twin marble staircases, Tiffany windows and Beaux-Arts design elements. Today, the Charles Street building hosts the Hotel Monaco. Its B&O American Brasserie was named after the building's railroad past.

LEFT *John Work Garrett was instrumental in the B&O Railroad's massive expansion during his tenure as president.*

OPPOSITE PAGE *The B&O Building was one of the many casualties of the 1904 fire that engulfed Baltimore.*

E. FRANCIS BALDWIN

The impressive first home downtown for the Baltimore & Ohio Railroad was designed by the railroad's chief architect, Ephraim Francis Baldwin. Born in Troy, New York, Baldwin was a son of a civil engineer. After his father's death, he and his mother returned to her hometown, Baltimore. In 1872, he was appointed as head architect for the B&O where he designed railroad stations, including Point of Rocks Station in Frederick County (above), the roundhouse building that now houses the B&O Railroad Museum in Baltimore and the B&O Warehouse, now part of the Camden Yards complex in Baltimore, home to the Baltimore Orioles. In addition to his work for the B&O, Baldwin also did considerable work for the Catholic Church, including St. Leo's Church and St. Ann's Church in Baltimore; the Shrine of the Sacred Heart in Mt. Washington; Theresa Hall at the College of Notre Dame Maryland; and St. Mary's Seminary.

Baltimore American Building BURNED 1904

For years, Baltimore experienced a spirited rivalry between two of its primary dailies, the *Baltimore Sun* and the *Baltimore American* (although several other newspapers have delved into the publishing business in Baltimore, see sidebar). Twenty-five years after the *Baltimore Sun* built its dramatic Sun Iron Building in 1850, its rival newspaper, the *Baltimore American* built an equally impressive new iron building … across the street. Situated on the southwest corner of Baltimore and South Streets downtown, the four-story building was designed by Thomas Dixon and Charles Carson and was completed in 1875. The iron fronted structure was designed in the Second Empire design with definite French influences.

Dramatic towers graced the roof's corners, and the design was well received by the downtown businesses, including the *Baltimore Sun*. According to a *Sun* article, the interiors were opulent, including the counting room, on the first floor, which was "lofty and richly ornamented … decorated in elegant taste, with paneled ceilings, frescoed walls, ornate cornices, and mahogany counter."

The erection of this ironclad building continued the popularity of the use of iron started by the Sun Iron Building with scores of other iron buildings being constructed along Baltimore Street. Sadly, like the Sun Iron Building, the Baltimore American building perished in the 1904 Great Baltimore Fire.

According to *Baltimore Afire* by Harold A. Williams in the immediate aftermath of the fire, the *Baltimore Sun* was published at the *Washington Evening Star*, and was printed in Washington, D.C., for two months after the fire. The *Sun* had made arrangements with the *Star* on February 7, 1904, and by 11:00 p.m., when it appeared the Sun Iron Building was doomed, the editorial, composing, and mail crews went by B&O train from Camden Station to Washington, D.C., to assemble the paper. The *Baltimore American,* however, did not print the day after the fire but was printed at the *Washington Times* for the following day's delivery. The *Baltimore News* and *Baltimore Herald* were both printed at the *Washington Post*. Due to high demand, newspapers that normally sold for a few cents sold for 25 cents in the days following the fire, according to Williams.

After the fire, the *American* was housed in the "American Building," which has the distinction of being the first office building constructed following the Great Baltimore Fire of 1904. The 14-story Beaux-Arts style skyscraper was built for General Felix Agnus, publisher of the *Baltimore American* newspaper, on the original site of its former headquarters.

There is much debate of the origins of the *Baltimore American*, although most agree that the likely origins date back to 1799 when Alexander Martin launched the *American and Daily Advertiser*. Over the years, the *Baltimore American* underwent a series of acquisitions and mergers, and as a result, name changes. At one time, the paper was owned by William Randolph Hearst, and for many years had the largest circulation in Baltimore, greater than its rival paper, the *Baltimore Sun,* which had the reputation of being the newspaper for the elite residents of Baltimore, while the *Baltimore American* and later the *News-American* was regarded more as the newspaper of the blue collar workers. The *Baltimore American,* the

morning newspaper, ceased publication in 1928 (although the Sunday paper still bore its name), and the *Baltimore News-American* closed its doors in 1986.

OPPOSITE PAGE *The Baltimore American building, seen in the center right of the photo, featured a cupola top.*

LEFT *The wrecked facade of the Baltimore American building following the Great Baltimore Fire of 1904.*

The Central Business Core **DESTROYED BY FIRE 1904**

The great Baltimore fire that erupted on the morning of February 7, 1904 destroyed more than 1,500 buildings that made up the 140-acre central business core in just over 48 hours. It caused an estimated $150 million in damage.

A small fire was first reported at the John Hurst & Co. building 10:48 a.m. and quickly spread. It soon became apparent that the fire was outstripping the ability of the city's firefighting resources, and calls for help were telegraphed to other cities. Fire departments from Washington, D.C., Atlantic City, Philadelphia, Wilmington, New York, Altoona, Pennsylvania, and other cities boarded special trains and headed to Baltimore. In all, a total of 57 engines, nine hook and ladder trucks, two hose companies and a fire boat battled the blaze.

The first outside units to arrive were from Washington, D.C., who arrived at 1:30 p.m. It was

MUSIC TO MY EARS

The great Baltimore fire was memorialized in a folk song entitled "Baltimore Fire." It was sung by Charlie Poole and the North Carolina Ramblers in a May 6, 1929 release by Columbia Records. The refrain went as follows:

Fire fire I heard the cry
From every breeze that passes by
All the world was one sad cry of pity
Strong men in anguish prayed
Calling out to the heavens for aid
While the fire in ruins was laid
Fair Baltimore the beautiful city

decided to attempt to halt the quickly spreading fire that was fed by high winds by implementing a firebreak, and the decision was made to raze existing buildings at the edge of the burning areas with dynamite. It was ultimately unsuccessful.

The fire raged from the morning of Sunday, February 7 through Monday, February 8, 1904. A total of 1,231 firefighters and 400 unattached volunteers were required to bring the blaze under control. High winds and freezing temperatures added to the difficulty for firefighters trying to contain the spread of flames. The fire burned over 30 hours, destroying 1,545 buildings spanning 70 city blocks. The open water of the Jones Falls was credited in stopping the flames as they moved eastward through the city.

In addition to firefighters, outside police officers, as well as the Maryland National Guard and the Naval Brigade, were utilized during the fire to maintain order and protect the city. Officers from Philadelphia and New York were sent to assist the Baltimore Police Department. Police and soldiers

ABOVE AND LEFT *Workers help clean out the street to make it passable.*

RIGHT *The intersection of Liberty and Lombard Streets, the southwest limit of the fire.*

were used to keep looters away and keep the fire zone free of civilians. The Naval Brigade secured the waterfront and waterways to keep spectators away.

A letter carrier and Baltimore native named Thomas Albert Lurz was honored by the U.S. Post Office for his efforts in rescuing tons of mail from the burning Central Post Office. Lurz assembled a group of men who loaded bags of mail onto horse drawn wagons and directed it on foot to North & Pennsylvania Avenues. They stood guard while the mail sat on the sidewalk until it could be protected by the National Guard.

Immediately after the fire, Mayor Robert McLane was quoted in the *Baltimore News* as saying, "To suppose that the spirit of our people will not rise to the occasion is to suppose that our people are not genuine Americans. We shall make

the fire of 1904 a landmark not of decline but of progress." He then refused federal assistance, stating, "As head of this municipality, I cannot help but feel gratified by the sympathy and the offers of practical assistance which have been tendered to us. To them I have in general terms replied, 'Baltimore will take care of its own, thank you.'" Two years later, on September 10, 1906, the *Baltimore Sun* reported that the city had risen from the ashes and "One of the great disasters of modern time had been converted into a blessing."

Miraculously, it was thought until recent history that the massive fire resulted in the loss of not a single life, likely due to the fact it started on a Sunday morning in the business core of the city. A historical marker that commemorates the Great Fire located next to the main entrance of the Port Discovery Children's Museum reads "Lives Lost:

ABOVE AND RIGHT *Streets covered in rubble hindered efforts to rebuild. Workers were brought in to clean up the ruins as the city attempted to rebuild.*

None." However, a recently discovered *Baltimore Sun* newspaper story from the time records that the "charred remains of a colored man" were pulled from the inner harbor, near the area where the USS *Constellation* was then docked, several days after the fire.

Five lost lives were attributed indirectly to the fire, including Martin Mullin, the proprietor of Mullin's Hotel, located on the northwest corner of Baltimore and Liberty Streets, just a block away from the start of the fire in the John Hurst & Co. building. In the aftermath, 35,000 people were left unemployed.

As a result of the fire a city building code was adopted. Public pressure, coupled with demands of companies insuring the newly re-built buildings, spurred the effort. The process took seventeen nights of hearings and multiple city council reviews.

The offices of noted writer H. L. Mencken at the *Baltimore Herald* newspaper were destroyed, but they printed an edition the first night of the fire on the press of the *Washington Post*. For the next five weeks the *Herald* was printed nightly on the press of the *Philadelphia Evening Telegraph* and transported 100 miles to Baltimore on a special train, provided free of charge by the Baltimore & Ohio Railroad.

Mencken recalls the fire and its aftermath in a chapter of his *Newspaper Days*, the second volume of his autobiography. He writes, "When I came out of it at last I was a settled and indeed almost a middle-aged man, spavined by responsibility and aching in every sinew, but I went into it a boy, and it was the hot gas of youth that kept me going."

Saloons and bars across the city had been closed since February 8th were allowed to reopen on February 15th, as long as "peace and order prevailed," or the drinking establishments would be promptly closed once again. Once the public was allowed into the burned out section of the city, business owners took the situation at heart, and began to convey their unfortunate situation through

OPPOSITE PAGE *These panoramic views show the extent of the devastation. The fire destroyed 1,500 buildings in just over 48 hours at a rate of 30 an hour.*

RIGHT *The Hurst Building, 15 minutes after the alarm.*

BELOW LEFT *Militia was called in to assist with crowd control and deter looters.*

BELOW RIGHT *Curious onlookers survey the damage on North Charles Street.*

humor. Signs read "Evicted Against Our Will" and "It Got Too Hot for Us Here—Call and See Us at Lexington and Park Avenues." Within two years, the area scorched by the fire had been completely rebuilt.

ABOVE LEFT *Firefighters try to tackle the blazes on Baltimore Street.*

ABOVE RIGHT *Downed power lines on Pratt and Light Streets complicated efforts to stop the fire.*

LEFT *Fire rages through the Guggenheimer & Weil building.*

RIGHT *Resilient Baltimore rebuilt the central business core within two years.*

Sun Iron Building BURNED 1904

The devastating Great Baltimore Fire of 1904 ravaged downtown Baltimore and its large path took down some of the city's most iconic and beautiful buildings. One such victim was the Sun Iron Building on Baltimore and South Streets, the impressive home of the *Baltimore Sun* newspaper.

The *Baltimore Sun*'s previous office was located not far away at Baltimore and Gay Streets; however, *Sun* proprietor Arunah S. Abell wanted a new building to house the sophisticated new printing equipment he purchased to accommodate the increased circulation the *Sun* was experiencing. According to architect and writer David G. Wright in the book, *Baltimore's Cast-Iron Buildings & Architectural Ironwork*, the budget for the new building was $100,000, more than double the customary budget set for commercial construction in an urban center at the time. In addition to the need for more space for printing presses, Abell also wanted a world-class, grand building downtown to showcase the newspaper's rise in prominence.

Abell and the *Baltimore Sun* took what was somewhat of a risky move by hiring a relative unknown builder for the project in James Bogardus of New York. Bogardus did not have a portfolio of commissioned work to showcase and his concept of an iron building was also revolutionary, especially for Baltimore at the time. The iron building would feature hundreds of dramatic windows, allowing for ample light, and the use of iron would protect—or so they thought—the building from fire. Robert Hatfield was hired as the architect, another bold move as most of his work was centered on residential design; however, he was experienced in the use of cast iron.

The Sun Iron Building began construction in 1850 and would be the largest all-iron structure in the United States when it was constructed. Besides its unique use of cast iron, the Sun Iron Building was also notable for its basement construction. Mimicking the *New York Sun*, Bogardus opted to have the printing presses located in the basement. In order to accommodate this desire, his design would have to extend beyond the property line on both Baltimore and South Streets by 23 feet. The reason for the foundation extension was to allow more underground area for the printing presses, a process that eventually would prove to be a disruption in traffic patterns downtown.

The Sun Iron Building also included hollow iron pipes that were installed through the surface of the sidewalks to provide fresh air to the basement, as well as the design element commonplace in New York City where thick glass disks are installed in the sidewalks to allow natural light to shine down to the basement area.

The bottom level of the Sun Iron Building contained commercial spaces that the *Sun* rented out to tenants ranging from a book publisher to a coal agent. Wright notes that the second floor was leased to three telegraph companies, which created the country's first communication center integrated with a newspaper. A sunburst clock and cupola were both added after construction was completed in 1851.

The Sun Iron Building's influence was felt in Baltimore, too. Abell's insistence that local ironworks companies be used—including Adam Denmead and Sons and Benjamin S. Benson— helped spur the ironworks industry in Baltimore, which at the time was more dominant in New York. According to Baltimore Heritage, Baltimore had over 100 cast iron buildings, but by 1962, the city was down to 36 buildings with cast iron fronts. With the advent of steel and new construction techniques at the turn of the 20th century, the use of architectural iron decreased sharply.

Despite the initial claims that the use of iron would protect the Sun Iron Building, the building perished in the Great Baltimore Fire of 1904, as when cast iron is exposed to intense heat, its structural properties diminish.

LEFT *Arunah Abell commissioned a cast iron building to house the newspaper's sophisticated printing equipment.*

RIGHT *Despite claims that iron would be resistant to burning, the Sun Iron Building perished in 1904.*

Montebello RAZED 1907

One of the many Baltimore's country estates located in the northern section of Baltimore City was Montebello, located on 33rd Street near The Alameda. Montebello was situated in the northeastern part of Baltimore and was built by one of George Washington's generals during the Revolutionary War, Samuel Smith, who would later serve as a U.S. Congressman for 40 years, U.S. Senator, Secretary of the Navy, and Mayor of Baltimore. In 1792, General Smith purchased 82 acres and began construction of a grand estate on the property. General Smith had fought alongside the French forces during the American Revolution and when he heard of the French victory over the Austrians in Montebello, Italy in 1800, he named his new estate Montebello in their honor. Over the years, Smith would acquire adjacent land and grow Montebello in size to over 600 acres.

In 1871, Montebello was purchased by Baltimore & Ohio Railroad President John Work Garrett. Garrett also owned a Gilded Age home set on 26 acres in Baltimore that is on the National Register of Historic Places. It is now a museum operated by Johns Hopkins University and houses over 50,000 of the family's belongings.

Under Garrett's ownership, Montebello grew from an already impressive 600 acres to almost 1,500 acres. In addition to the large mansion, Montebello boasted a greenhouse, stone quarry, private racetrack, and stables that provided stalls for almost 200 horses.

Montebello was especially important to John Work Garrett in his latter years as the large country estate and its rural surroundings allowed for quiet reflection, in-home meetings with B&O Railroad executives, and for him to tend to his ailing health. In 1883, his beloved wife died at Montebello. A November 18, 1883 obituary in *The New York Times,* stated:

Mrs. John W. Garrett died at Montebello yesterday morning at 8:10 o'clock, unconscious and without suffering. The injuries she received while out riding on Oct. 11 resulted in acute inflammation of the brain, which was the immediate cause of death. In falling from the carriage, Mrs. Garrett struck her head upon the road with great force, causing concussion of the brain from which she became unconscious, and so remained during the greater part of her illness. She was surrounded by all her family when she died. The coachman who was driving Mrs. Garrett had been driving her for many years, and was very much trusted by her, and her horses which she had used in that occasion were those she had been driving for some years past.

Devastated by the loss of his wife, John W. Garrett died the following year in his Deer Park home; his estate was valued at $5.6 million upon his death. Garrett's funeral took place at Montebello, as indicated by a September 29, 1884 obituary in *The New York Times:*

The funeral of the late John W. Garrett took place to-day from Montebello, the country residence of the deceased. The services, in accordance with the expressed desire of Mr. Garrett during his illness, were of the simplest character … A very large number of the relatives and friends of the family were assembled at Montebello at 9 o'clock. After the reading of the burial service …the remains were taken to Green Mount Cemetery, the funeral cortege comprising upward of 150 carriages. Within and outside the cemetery walls fully 12,000 persons were gathered to pay their last tribute of respect to the deceased.

In 1907, Montebello was demolished for the construction of 33rd Street, although the barn and racing stables outlasted the main mansion for several years before also succumbing to development plans for the Ednor Gardens neighborhood by the E.J. Gallagher Realty Company.

LEFT *Montebello was constructed on 82 acres of north Baltimore, in what is now 33rd Street.*

OPPOSITE PAGE *B&O President John Work Garrett expanded the property several times during his ownership and added stables for 200 horses.*

Union Station RAZED 1910

Each day, thousands of passengers pass through Baltimore's Pennsylvania Station. What they may not realize is that Penn Station, as it's more commonly known, is the third railroad station to be situated on the site.

Until 1928, Baltimore's station was called Union Station. In 1873, a wooden station was built by the Northern Central Railway. The original station was small and was remodeled in 1882 to permit all trains of the Northern Central, the Philadelphia, Wilmington and Baltimore, the Union, the Western Maryland, and the Baltimore and Potomac railroads to pass through the same terminus. The original station was replaced in 1886 by a more substantial brick structure featuring a mansard roof and situated below street level. The new station was built by the Pennsylvania Railroad, which had purchased the Northern Central Railway.

A December 30, 1885 article in the *Baltimore Sun* outlined the construction efforts of the new brick station:

A broad, easy stairway leads from the bridge platform down to the large waiting-room in the station. This room is 110 feet long, 50 feet wide and the ceiling is 26 feet in height. The room will be wainscoted in chestnut and will be handsomely decorated and furnished. When the new station is ready for business, the old frame building now in use will be torn down.

The article also mentioned how the construction of the new station had served as an impetus for construction of fine houses close by. Cost to build the new station was estimated at $150,000 and Baltimore sand brick would be used for the exterior. The three-story station was said to be second in grandeur behind Philadelphia's Broad Street station, and that all the bricks, lumber, terra cotta, and nearly every piece of material would be from Baltimore.

The new brick station would soon fall out of favor with Baltimore residents. A January 20, 1908 *Baltimore Sun* article called on the Pennsylvania Railroad to build an adequately sized station:

The station is too small for the business it is intended to accommodate. The city has outgrown its capacity ... the passengers' quarters have become greatly cramped and wholly unworthy of the needs of a city of Baltimore's size.

The editorial also complained about the lack of elevators for invalids or cripples, lack of covering for passengers as they walked to the right track, exposing them to inclement weather, and insufficient staffing for luggage and ticket taking. Baltimoreans also noted that there were far superior stations in nearby Harrisburg, Pennsylvania, Philadelphia, and Wilmington, Delaware.

Most disturbing was that passengers risked their lives by crossing tracks to catch their train. Over the years, many passengers were killed or injured attempting to catch their trains. "The company has been promising a new station for many years, but the fulfillment of that promise is apparently as far away now as it was years ago," noted a newspaper editorial.

Finally, in late 1908 and early 1909, news broke that the new, modern station that Baltimore had been clamoring for was finally going to happen.

Union Station was demolished in 1910 to make way for a new Beaux-Arts station that remains today. And while the former brick station was razed, other railroad buildings in Baltimore have been repurposed. The Baltimore and Ohio Railroad's Camden warehouse was incorporated into Camden Yards, while the B&O's Mount Royal station was restored for studio space for the Maryland Institute College of Art.

In 1928, Baltimore's Union Station was renamed Pennsylvania Station. In 2004, an enormous new statue was installed in the front roundabout. The 50-plus-foot-tall sculpture features a male and female body form intersected with an LED heart light that changes colors from blue to red to black.

LEFT *This 1906 postcard shows the original Union Station, which was razed in 1910 for the construction of Penn Station.*

RIGHT *The elegant Union Station was heavily criticized for its lack of safety and inadequate size for the booming railroad business.*

Political Conventions CEASED 1912

Chicago holds the title of the city that has hosted the most political conventions for the two current major parties, but some would be surprised to learn that Baltimore has hosted 20 conventions in its history, although many of them were for parties that are no longer in existence or third-party conventions. The last major convention held in Baltimore was in 1912. Due to its reputation for being located in a pretty solid "blue state" and a very solid Democratic city, it's unlikely that Baltimore will be used anytime soon for a convention, as today's conventions are typically held in states that are key swing states.

Due to its easy access to railroad lines and steamships, plus its convention halls and well-known hotels, Baltimore was a popular choice in the early years of political conventions. In fact, Baltimore hosted 10 of the first 11 national gatherings, including all three of the conventions held before the 1832 presidential election. In all, six future presidents have been nominated at conventions held in Baltimore.

Of the many conventions held in Baltimore, some particularly stand out for historical importance as well as oddity. The first-ever political convention was actually held in Baltimore in 1831. Fueled by a need for a more democratic process for nominating candidates—presidential candidates used to be selected by state legislatures or Congressional caucuses—the first "third party" was formed, and in 1831 it held the first convention in Baltimore. The Anti-Masonic Party, suspicious of the perceived influence of the Masons, was formed, and on September 25, 1831, its delegates met in Baltimore and chose Marylander William Wirt, a former U.S. attorney general, as its nominee. Wirt won only one state, Vermont, in the 1832 election won easily by Andrew Jackson for his second term. The Anti-Masonic Party soon folded.

That same election year, the two major parties also held their conventions in Baltimore. In 1832, the first Democratic convention nominated Andrew Jackson, while the Republicans nominated Henry Clay of Kentucky. The Democratic Convention is notable as the party formally adopted its present name, and the party refused to re-nominate John C. Calhoun of South Carolina as its vice president candidate, primarily over Calhoun's support of a state's right to nullify federal law within its borders, a foreshadowing to the ugly slavery battle that would ensue in later years. The Democratic Convention was also noteworthy as it started the procedure where one person from each delegation would announce the vote of his or her state.

The 1835 Democratic Convention was held a year and a half before the election as the party wanted to ensure that President Jackson's handpicked successor, Martin Van Buren, would be the nominee. In 1840, the Democrats held their convention in Baltimore again and issued its first-ever party platform. That same year in Baltimore, the Whig Party Convention was held in Baltimore with William Henry Harrison and John Tyler nominated for president and vice president respectively, complete with a parade to the Canton Race Track. Unlike today, candidates then did not attend their own nominating conventions.

Baltimore was also the site of the controversial convention of 1844 where James K. Polk, a relative unknown Congressman who had attended the convention with the hope of landing the vice presidential spot, was nominated for president in a surprise move by the party, as Martin Van Buren was considered the favorite. However, Polk's stock rose with his support of the annexation of Texas, a

BALTIMORE CONVENTION·

popular party platform that year, while Van Buren opposed annexation of the Lone Star State. Polk went on to defeat Henry Clay for president. Four years later, Clay, who had vowed to serve only one term and would die shortly after leaving office, was not on the ticket, and the Democrats' convention was a contentious one, with the issue of whether slavery should be banned in the new western territories won from Mexico. Lewis Cass was nominated for the Democrats in Baltimore, the convention was a disaster, and Martin Van Buren of the Whig party won the presidency that year.

If the Democrat Party thought its 1848 convention was a tumultuous one, 1860 would prove to truly test the party's unity. The party first met in Charleston, South Carolina, where a heated dispute between the party's northern and southern state delegates broke out with several southern delegates walking out of the convention. While the party did not nominate a candidate in Charleston, it did confirm its support of the Supreme Court's Dred Scott decision that prohibited slavery in the territories. In June of that year, the Democrats convened in Baltimore with a sparsely attended convention and nominated Stephen A. Douglas for president. However, Southern Democrats again walked out over the dispute over slavery and nominated Vice President John C. Breckinridge of Kentucky while supporting slavery in the new territories. Republican Abraham Lincoln won the election.

Four years later during the Civil War, Lincoln was nominated for a second term at the National Union Party in Baltimore; the name was a nod to the Democrats who had supported Lincoln's war policy. Florida and Virginia delegates were allowed to attend but not vote, while South Carolina's delegates were denied attendance. Lincoln easily won the nomination with Andrew Johnson, a Democrat, chosen as his running mate.

The Democrats returned to Baltimore in 1872 in the shortest convention in history—six hours. The party did not endorse a candidate; instead it endorsed the presidential and vice presidential candidates of the Liberal Republican Party in an attempt to defeat Ulysses S. Grant.

The last major political convention held in Baltimore was in 1912 as the Democrats held theirs at the Fifth Regiment Armory Building where they nominated Woodrow Wilson, governor of New Jersey, for president. William Jennings Bryan's endorsement of Wilson is seen as a pivotal moment for Wilson.

In 2012, the Green Party held its convention in Baltimore where Jill Stein, a Massachusetts physician, beat out actress Roseanne Barr for the nomination.

ABOVE *William Jennings Bryan, who ran unsuccessfully for president, attends the nomination of Woodrow Wilson for president. Wilson appointed Bryan Secretary of State.*

LEFT *The Fifth Regiment Armory, which was built for the 1912 Convention on the site of the Bolton estate.*

OPPOSITE PAGE *Photo taken at the 1912 Democratic National Convention held at the Fifth Regiment Armory.*

Electric Park RAZED 1916

Like other amusement parks in Baltimore, including River View Park, Electric Park afforded city residents in the late 19th and early 20th century the chance to escape everyday life, enjoy thrilling rides, hear live music, and spend quality time with family and friends. However, Electric Park did have an element that other parks did not possess. Featuring thousands of incandescent lights, Electric Park shined brightly on Belvedere Avenue, as revelers streamed to the park to marvel at the light display upon opening in the 1890s. Being used to the softer, dimmer candlelight and gas light fixtures, these new electric lights, still a novelty in the late 19th century, were shockingly bright.

Electric Park was set on 24 acres in northwest Baltimore and opened in 1896 as a horse race track. The owners and management hoped that Electric Park would be to Maryland what Coney Island was to New York. Electric Park touted a carousel, two roller coasters, boat lake, swimming pool, and live entertainment. Some of the more odd attractions included a simulation of the horrific Johnstown Flood, the 1889 disaster in Pennsylvania when a dam failure released 20 million tons of water, causing $17 million in damages and killing over 2,000 people. Another unique ride was the Human Laundry Ride, allowing ride goers the experience of what it would feel like to go through a clothes-washing cycle.

Electric Park was also the first place in Maryland to show a motion picture to the public, and, in 1900, it was the home to the state's first automobile race.

In 1907, in a drive to further boost attendance, Electric Park started the Greater Electric Park Fair, a two-week agricultural and textile fair to rival the Maryland State Fair held in Timonium in Baltimore County. Fair organizers counted on Electric Park's closer proximity to the city center than Timonium as an impetus for large crowds. In addition to exhibits, the Greater Electric Park Fair featured band concerts in the afternoon, and orchestra, dancing,

and vaudeville performances at night, as well as roller-skating. The fair also dedicated one day to politicians, inviting all Democrat and Republican politicians to attend the same day to allow the citizenry the opportunity to meet them and ask questions. In an effort to drive attendees, the United Railways and Electric Company ran the Linden Avenue streetcars all the way to the fairgrounds.

A May 1907 *Baltimore Sun* article describes the park's thousands of incandescent lights and wide range of amusements. One of the more popular attractions was a high-diver, who plunged from 120 feet high into a shallow tank of water and a "fire dive in which Oscar Norin leaps from the tower a sheet of flame and plunges into a blazing tank."

Another *Baltimore Sun* article from 1908 reported that the manager of the Electric Park Company had been arrested on charges of assault after he entered the park, assaulted an employee, and pulled a pistol. A receiver had recently been appointed under claims that the park was being mismanaged and was financially insolvent. The landowner who leased the land to Electric Park claimed that he was owed $344.14 for electric current supplied at the park.

In 1910, Electric Park was purchased by August Fenneman, owner of a vaudeville theatre, who planned to spend $75,000 on improvements, including a double-decked movable stage and a larger swimming pool. The new owner added a restaurant and lured away the chef from the Hotel Waldorf-Astoria in New York. The park also expanded its schedule to be open year round and added such attractions as a trapeze act, a Mexican dog show, and a Wild West cowboy and Indian performance.

Electric Park survived many other challenges, such as an 1896 hurricane that blew down all the fences, lifted the roof off the casino, and broke many windows, and a fire in 1904 that destroyed the clubhouse, deck and grotto and caused $40,000 in damages. Electric Park was also raided in 1914 due to selling liquor without a license. The following year, however, Electric Park closed and it was razed in 1916.

LEFT *The aptly named Electric Park drew tourists from around the Mid-Atlantic region.*

ABOVE *Electric Park was set on a 24-acre plot.*

RIGHT *To boost attendance for the annual fair, streetcar lines were extended to the park.*

German Breweries SHUT DOWN 1920

The story of Baltimore's many brewing companies is complex and often interwoven as brands and companies merged, split, and renamed themselves. Mostly owned by German-born families, they ranged from small brewing operations to vast complexes of bottling plants and breweries capable of producing hundreds of thousands of barrels each year. Germans had immigrated to Baltimore mostly due to the European Revolutions of 1848 that adversely affected the stability of states that would become modern day Germany. To encourage the communal and continual drinking of beer, they also established a multitude of beer gardens throughout the city. The Zion Lutheran Church on East Lexington Street was founded by the increasingly wealthy Germans, and was known locally as the "Brewer's Church."

When John F. Wiessner opened his brewery in 1863, for example, there were already 21 breweries operating in Baltimore City and nearby sections of Baltimore County. The area Wiessner chose for his brewery was close to a brewery built in 1853 by George Rost and they would be joined shortly, in 1864, by the George Bauerschmidt brewery. George B. and Fred Bauerschmidt were brothers who ran competing breweries in Baltimore. The area around North Gay Street would prove to be a popular location for myriad Baltimore breweries.

Wiessner was born in 1831 in Bavaria, the son of a brewer. He came to Baltimore in 1853 and worked as a brewmaster in the Rost Brewery. He desired a brewery of his own, but lacked sufficient funds. He returned to Bavaria in 1862 and convinced family members to invest in his Baltimore brewery. He leased the land, and built his three-story brewery, which fronted on Belle Air Avenue (now Gay Street).

Wiessner built his large house on the property, and provided board and lodging for brewery workers, many who had recently emigrated from Germany. By 1886, output was about 40,000 barrels per year.

Just a block to the south, George Bauerschmidt began building a replacement brewery of his own that year, at a time when his brother Fred began his own brewery. Just to the north, the former Rost Brewery, renamed Standard Brewery, was also modernizing.

In 1901, 16 Baltimore brewers consolidated themselves into the Gottlieb-Bauerschmidt-Straus Brewing Company, including Maryland Brewing Co., and the Globe Brewery. In 1921, the company changed its name to the Globe Brewing & Mfg. Company, a maker of the popular Arrow Beer.

Wiessner and Fred Bauerschmidt stayed independent breweries, but all eventually joined what had become the Brewery Trust. Growing anti-German sentiment during World War I foreshadowed the inevitable demise of German named brewing companies.

The 1920 Volsted Act meant that all the breweries in the country closed due to prohibition. Many were converted into ice cream and ice factories until repeal of prohibition in 1926. Beer returned to Baltimore, but corporate consolidations and improvements in interstate shipping and refrigeration meant that beer could be brewed thousands of miles away in more efficient plants.

LEFT *The American Brewery, built in 1887, was an active brewery until 1973. The building remains and has recently been rehabilitated for the use by a non-profit organization.*

ABOVE *The Bauerschmidt brewery opened in 1864, joining other well-known German breweries in Baltimore.*

RIGHT *Not all breweries were housed in large factories; some were located in converted townhouses.*

Northern Baltimore Estate Houses

DEMOLISHED FROM 1920s

As Baltimore's population grew in size in the late 20th century, its real estate developers began to purchase the dozens of vast country estates to the north of the city with the intent of razing the houses and developing the grounds into new suburban communities. Ornate gardens, orchards, mansions, outbuildings, and agriculture fields were razed and replaced with rows of row houses such as those found in the Charles Village neighborhood. Others were purchased and developed into new neighborhoods with large houses like Guilford. Some of these lost grand estates included Guilford, Ulman, and the Wyman Villa.

The estate known as Guilford was originally the country estate of General McDonald, who named his house to commemorate the battle of Guilford Court House, North Carolina. His son, William, upon inheriting the estate about 1850, built the old Guilford Mansion, located where 4001 Greenway Road is today. William McDonald bred and raced horses at the vast estate, including Flora Temple, once the fastest horse in the United States. During the Civil War he was imprisoned at Fort McHenry for allowing southern sympathizers to signal messages to the Confederate troops in Anne Arundel County from the tower of the Guilford Mansion.

McDonald's widow married John De Speyer, who sold the estate in 1872 to Arunah S. Abell, founder of *The Sun* newspaper. It remained in the Abell family for 35 years, until 1907, when it was sold to the Guilford Park Company, who soon consolidated with the Roland Park Company. The mansion was razed in 1914 to make way for the development of the Guilford neighborhood.

Some of the early estates remained far after they had become surrounded by the row houses built in the 20th century. One of these was the large Ulman estate, with its mansion built sometime between 1871 and 1879 by wealthy liquor merchant Alfred J. Ulman. Although it comprised a much larger property, when the grid pattern of streets was laid out in Charles Village, the house became known as 2801 North Charles Street.

A.J. Ulman, as he was known, was born in Germany in 1830 and immigrated 20 years later aboard the SS *Esperanza*. He and 16 other individuals were recorded in the house and its many outbuildings in the 1880 census. In addition to his wife Clementine and their four children, the family also had a live-in cook, maid, gardener, nurse, coachman, several servants and even a resident florist.

Cardinal Gibbons and Father Wade of the Saints Philip and James Church bought the Ulman mansion from a subsequent owner on March 20, 1920, for an astonishing $111,680.75. They rented the house for a while to the University School for Boys, also known as Marston's Academy. The house was razed in 1927 to make way for the construction of the present-day church and rectory.

Prosperous wholesale dry goods merchant Samuel G. Wyman had purchased the Carroll family's estate coined Homewood House in 1839, still extant on today's Hopkins college campus. He decided he wanted a new house built for himself on its vast grounds after viewing designs by well-known architect Richard Upjohn that appeared in the popular book of the day, *Architecture of Country Houses* by Andrew Jackson Downing.

Wyman found a local draftsman to replicate the design from the book. Completed in 1853, the Italianate-style villa closely replicated the Upjohn original because Wyman had hired a Newport, Rhode Island carpenter who had worked on the original design, built for Edward King. His son, William Wyman, lived in the house until 1903.

Concerned that his estate would be bought by local developers and divided up, Wyman had earlier, in 1898, donated his 60-acre estate to the financially strapped Johns Hopkins University for relocation of its campus, and an area known as the Dell for use as a park. Johns Hopkins University razed the Wyman Villa in 1954, but its elaborate gatehouse exists today, located at the corner of North Charles Street and Art Museum Drive, serving as the school's newsletter office.

ABOVE *The home of Johns Hopkins on West Saratoga Street was modest when considering Hopkins' vast fortune.*

RIGHT *Prosperous wholesale dry goods merchant Samuel G. Wyman constructed an Italianate-style villa in 1853.*

RIGHT *Samuel G. Wyman's villa was razed in 1954 by Johns Hopkins University.*

010905. OYSTER LUGGERS AT THE DOCKS, BALTIMORE, MD.

Federal Hill Industry DIMINISHED 1921

Locals and tourists alike descend on Federal Hill on weekends—families during the day to climb the historic Civil War hill site and make their way over to Ft. McHenry; locals shop for fresh produce at Cross Street Market; young couples enjoy romantic dinners at one of the many casual and high-end restaurants that dot Charles and Light Streets; while young revelers bar hop throughout the neighborhood's many bars and clubs geared toward those in their 20s and 30s.

The neighborhood's housing stock is some of the most expensive in Baltimore City, which makes it even more difficult to imagine how this young, urban neighborhood known for its shopping and entertainment was once the hub of factories and industrial centers dedicated to some of the more unattractive industries.

Federal Hill has been home to many different industries including glass making (sand was mined from Federal Hill itself), breweries, paint manufacturers, and large-scale bakeries, but the neighborhood's waterfront location and proximity to shipping piers made it a natural for seafood production. One of the most influential industries in Federal Hill was oyster canning, an industry that took hold in Baltimore in the 1820s and 1830s. The proximity of the Chesapeake Bay's oyster beds, and the efficient railroad system in place gave Baltimore the tools to thrive in the oyster canning business, and by the late 19th century, over 100 canneries were present, many of which employed newly arrived immigrants, primarily from Eastern Europe.

One of the pioneers in oyster canning was Thomas Kensett, who in the 1820s was canning oysters in New York and was granted the patent on tin cans. Kensett and his son brought the oyster canning business to Baltimore in the 1850s, setting up shop in Federal Hill. Baltimore quickly became the leading oyster canning location in the United States, if not the world. Other oyster canning companies included William Numsen and Company, Moore & Brady, and Platt and Company Oyster Packers, whose plant location is now the home of the Baltimore Museum of Industry on Key Highway.

According to Norman Rukert in the book *Federal Hill*, fertilizer was also a key industry in Federal Hill. One of the first fertilizing companies was started by William Davison, who settled in Baltimore in 1826 from Ireland. According to Rukert, he started a business with John Kettlewell on what is now Riverside Avenue. They advertised themselves as "Grinders and Acidulators of Old Bones and Oyster Shells." The bones and shells were used to make phosphoric acid, a key ingredient of fertilizer.

Other early pioneers in the industry included Ober and Kettlewell, R.W.L. Rasin and Company, and the Maryland Fertilizing and Manufacturing Company.

Other manufacturing and chemical plants operated in Federal Hill in the mid- to late 19th centuries, including an Epsom salt plant, furnace companies, and various iron and steel mills.

While most of these manufacturing companies were gone from Federal Hill by the turn of the 20th century, one large nearby factory is still in existence today—the world-famous Domino Sugar factory, whose massive neon light still shines down on Federal Hill today.

LEFT *Baltimore was once America's oyster canning capital.*

OPPOSITE PAGE *The array of shipping piers in and around the Inner Harbor and the easy access to the Chesapeake Bay made neighborhoods like Federal Hill natural epicenters of the seafood industry.*

Riverview Park RAZED 1929

Today, tourists from around the world descend on Baltimore's Inner Harbor to enjoy the scenic views, Maryland blue crabs, the world-famous National Aquarium, the Maryland Science Center, as well as a water taxi to Ft. McHenry, a battle site of the War of 1812 where Francis Scott Key penned "The Star-Spangled Banner." Until its closing in early 2012, tourists—and locals alike—could also take part in an old-fashioned carousel ride at the Inner Harbor. For years, though, if Baltimoreans wanted to take a thrilling roller coaster ride, they needed to make a trip to Ocean City, Maryland, or to one of the amusement parks in neighboring states such Busch Gardens in Virginia.

However, in the late 19th and early 20th century, several amusement parks were located in the heart of Baltimore City, including Electric Park and Riverview Park. Located at Point Breeze near the neighborhood of Canton in East Baltimore, Riverview Park had an unimpressive start as a small beer garden in 1868. According to Norman G. Rukert in his book *Historic Canton*, the beer garden was started by John Lowery as a one-story red brick building shaded by trees and was known as "Lowery's Place on Colgate Creek." It was sold in the 1870s to Harry McGowan, and, according to Rukert, "McGowan apparently had a flair for publicity; he planted 100 trees around his property, naming them for friends, and kept two black bears, which were famous for the amount of beer they could drink."

Eventually the park was sold in 1898 to the City and Suburban Railway, and it was renamed Riverview Park and amusement rides were added. Vintage postcards show how Riverview Park was billed as, "The Coney Island of the South."

Riverview Park featured roller coaster rides, a "Human Roulette Wheel," roller rink, rides, a "Tunnel of Love," as well as live entertainment, such as a circus and the Royal Artillery Band of Italy, which drew up to 60,000 spectators. Also a popular draw was the fireworks display on Independence Day. Due to its ideal waterfront location, visitors could also enjoy swimming in the Patapsco River, the perfect way to cool off on a hot summer day in a time when community swimming pools were not as commonplace as today. Bathers could take a refreshing swim and then dry off while being whisked around on one of the many carnival rides.

However, the highlight of the park was the famous roller coaster ride, which Rukert says was the first one in the South. According to Rukert, those who rode the roller coaster were greeted with the following call by the conductor: "Hold your hats, false teeth, wooden legs, glass eyes, powder puffs, and chewing gum!"

Despite its success, Riverview Park was besieged by more than one fire, most notably the 1909 fire that ravaged the park. Riverview Park did reopen in 1910, although not to the crowds it was accustomed to, and in 1915, another fire struck. In addition to the fires, a 1961 *Baltimore Sun* article also noted that Prohibition played a role in the demise of Riverview Park.

In 1929, Riverview Park was bought at auction by Western Electric, an electric engineering company and the manufacturing arm of AT&T, and the amusement rides were sold off.

ABOVE *A 1914 postcard of the bandstand at Riverview Park, which could draw 60,000 spectators for concerts.*

RIGHT *Riverview Park's location adjacent to the Patapsco River allowed visitors to cool off after the amusement rides.*

BELOW *In 1898, the City and Suburban Railway purchased the park and added amusement rides.*

Brick Facades COVERED WITH PERMA-STONE 1930s

For decades, roving salesmen for simulated stone companies like Perma-Stone or Formstone convinced tens of thousands of Baltimore homeowners to cover their old brick facades with their newly invested product. They made a hefty commission for each sale, and Baltimore became known for its rows upon rows of Perma-Stone clad row houses. Simulated stone has been on the market since 1929.

"Simulated masonry" covers many common trade names of mostly cement-based materials applied to a wall surface and manipulated to create a faux stone appearance. Similar to stucco, this multiple layered covering was commonly scored to simulate mortar joints, colored to create individual

'stones,' and sometimes even finished with mica chips to create a stone like reflection on a sunny day. It could take on the look of everything from rounded stones to small granite blocks or layers of slate. In most cases, it's a multi-layered cement material applied to a wire net or lath attached to an existing brick facade.

The most common manufacturer was perhaps Perma-Stone, a catchy name that has taken on a generic term referring to myriad products installed by a variety of manufacturers and trained craftsman over the past 75 years. Others included Formstone, Rostone, Tru-Stone, Fieldstone, Bermuda Stone, Modern Stone, Romanstone, Magnolia Stone, Dixie Stone, and Silverstone. Perma-Stone is still

manufactured to this day. The application not only covered up the brick facade of the house, it usually called for removing window and door trim, capstones, brackets, and other decorative features of row houses.

According to Baltimore resident and film director John Waters, faux stone is "the polyester of brick" as visitors to Baltimore might soon understand while walking down block after block of

OPPOSITE PAGE *Baltimore is well known for its rows and rows of brick homes.*

BELOW *While many homes retain their brick facades, a large percentage have been covered with Perma-Stone.*

early 19th-century row houses covered with a variety of simulated stone. In most cases, that product would be Formstone, patented by Baltimore resident Albert Knight in 1937 for his 'Lasting Products Company.' Its use was so widespread in Baltimore that in 1997 it became the subject of a 30-minute documentary film entitled *Little Castles: A Formstone Phenomenon* by Lillian Bowers & Skizz Cyzyk. The Formstone story is told by the men and women who made it, sold it, bought it, and installed it. The idea for the documentary had come when Bowers herself had dreamed that the gravestone of her grandfather was being covered with Formstone.

Utilized for about 75 years, simulated masonry can trace its beginnings to 1929 in Ohio, with numerous manufacturers in the 1930s and 1940s rapidly copying what was a successful product, much desired by both old homeowners and those building new homes. The concept is nothing new, as early builders in America often simulated stone quoins and wall surfaces utilizing sand-infused paint over wood, often carved to replicate the beveled edges of a stone block.

The Perma-Stone name was registered as a trademark in 1929 by the Perma-Stone Company in Columbus, Ohio, who provided molds and materials necessary for the installation through trained and authorized local dealers. Its immediate success spurned many other competitors interested in filling the desire for the stone aesthetic and the need for a 'maintenance free' covering over poorly constructed or deteriorating exterior walls.

The original intended use of Formstone, patented in 1937, was to apply a uniform exterior covering over a suburban house that had undergone additions with unmatched siding materials. It quickly became used to cover the exterior surfaces of older row houses, however, plagued with penetrating moisture from the use of inferior brick.

The introduction of simulated stone products in the 1930s helped to serve the needs of changing aesthetics throughout America. Americans have traditionally sought the latest in building materials to cover up older outdated material, to yearn for a maintenance-free exterior covering, or to convey the look of an expensive masonry exterior at a modest price.

With the inferior porous quality of brick used for the construction of tens of thousands of row houses in Baltimore, for example, the sealing qualities and advertised maintenance-free, 20-year guarantee of Formstone was seen as an end-all to a lifetime problem of leaking walls and peeling paint. Its salesmen promised that for the cost of three paint jobs, their maintenance worries would be over for good.

Many religious institutions utilized simulated stone products to make extentions and additional buildings match the style of their real stone churches. Application seems to have reached its zenith in the 1950s, but lost popularity by the 1970s when aluminum and vinyl siding could be applied at a much cheaper cost.

WORTHY OF PRESERVATION?

For some time now, the concept of simulated masonry as worthy of preservation has crept into some historic district guidelines, while others prohibit its use. The Hampden Village Main Street Program in Baltimore states, "While Formstone removal may also be included as a facade improvement, applicants are encouraged to keep Formstone that is in good condition as it is a distinctive part of Baltimore's unique heritage." At the same time, however, Perma-Stone in particular is not allowed on a St. Louis City Landmark. Many real estate agents readily advertise a stoned exterior as a maintenance free and added value feature to the structure. It's a debate that will likely continue into the future as 20th-century materials leave their mark, so to speak, on the landscape of America.

LEFT *Some homeowners were concerned by the porous nature of brick and looked for alternative coverings.*

RIGHT *Population increases necessitated the erection of Baltimore's many narrow row homes.*

Enoch Pratt Library and Latrobe Block

RAZED 1931

The Enoch Pratt Library system in Baltimore is one of the oldest library systems in the country. Today's large central location on Cathedral Street was preceded by a Romanesque style building with a central tower that served as the library's initial main location.

Enoch Pratt, who was born in Massachusetts in 1808, grew up with modest means as his family were farmers. He arrived in Baltimore with only $150 to his name but quickly became a successful businessman as an iron commission merchant, and later, he became vice president of the Philadelphia, Wilmington, and Baltimore Railroad, director of Susquehanna Canal Company, and president of the National Farmers' and Planters' Bank of Baltimore.

Pratt's successful business career allowed him to engage in significant philanthropic endeavors, most notably, funding the establishment of Baltimore's public library system. Learning of the need for a public library, Pratt approached the mayor and city council offering funding for not only the construction of a central library downtown but also a large endowment to maintain the library. Pratt's gift in 1882 was in excess of $1 million—

$225,000 of that would be used to construct the library, while the balance would be used as an endowment to maintain the library in the future.

Charles Carson was selected as the architect, and he chose a Romanesque Revival design with arched windows, white marble for the exterior, and large imposing pillars at the entrance. Busts of famous men were used as design elements, and the entrance was situated above street level.

The library opened in 1886 to much fanfare as lines streamed down the block each morning at opening time. Library patrons had to look up book titles and then request them from a clerk, as the library stacks were closed. A reading room was located on the second floor.

Within three months of the opening of the Central Library, four branches were opened— Branch 3 at Light and Gittings Streets, Branch 2 at Hollins and Calhoun Streets, Branch 1 at Freemont and Pitcher Streets, and Branch 4 at Canton and O'Donnell Streets. The Canton branch remains today. That same year, Harry S. Cummings became the first African-American to get a Pratt Library card.

Although Baltimore's citizens loved the new library, architectural critics were not as kind. Writers for *The Evening Sun* lambasted its design and called for its destruction. Critics found the design gloomy and boring, a stark contrast to the elegant residential buildings in the Mount Vernon neighborhood at the time.

Despite the sometimes-harsh criticism for its design, the Pratt Library flourished. By 1894, less than 10 years after opening, the Pratt Library was one of the largest in the country. In fact, according to the Enoch Pratt Library, only three public libraries (Boston, Chicago, and Cincinnati) had larger book

collections, and only three libraries (Boston, Chicago, and New York) had higher circulation counts. At the onset of the 20th century, Andrew Carnegie gave $500,000 in order for the Pratt Library to build 20 new library branches, furthering access to Baltimore residents living outside of the downtown area. In 1908, the library received its first financial appropriation by The City of Baltimore.

However, over the years, the Central Library was starting to show its age, and the library's collections were testing the physical space limitations of Carson's original building. In 1927, Baltimore voters overwhelmingly approved a $3 million loan to build a new Central Library building. Pratt Library staff and 400,000 volumes of work were moved to a temporary space at Redwood Street and Hopkins Place. In 1931, the original library was demolished for a larger building to be erected on the same land. The new building remains today.

In addition to the razing of the library, several houses designed by Benjamin Henry Latrobe, who designed the U.S. Capitol and the Baltimore Basilica, were also demolished to make way for the new library building.

LEFT *One of the houses designed by Benjamin Henry Latrobe that was also demolished in 1931 to make way for the new Enoch Pratt Library.*

RIGHT *Self-made millionaire Enoch Pratt established Baltimore's public library system.*

OPPOSITE PAGE *The inability to accommodate a growing collection led to the demise of Central Library.*

Canvas Window Awnings

DISCONTINUED 1940s

In 19th century Baltimore and other cities, residents could have directed visitors to their house by mentioning the color of their exterior window awnings, as virtually every house had them on their facade. They were mounted above windows, doors, and porches, and provided shade from the blistering summer sun long before air-conditioning was introduced.

Awnings were first used by the ancient Egyptian and Syrian civilizations, who described them as "woven mats" that shaded market stalls and homes. They could also be hazardous at times, as Roman poet Lucretius wrote in 50 BC: "Linen-awning, stretched, over mighty theatres, gives forth at times, a cracking roar, when much 'tis beaten about, betwixt the poles and cross-beams."

It is believed that sailors, with their background in sail making and rigging, were the first to adapt sailcloth on wooden frames to be mounted above a window or door for protection from the rain and sun. The advent of the steamship forced canvas mills and sail makers to search for new markets.

By the late 1800s specialized awning hardware was developed, which spurred the use of awnings for homes and businesses. The fabric was laced on, permitting a better fit and look, and the awning covers could easily be taken down in the winter and reinstalled when spring arrived. At the same time advances were being made in painting the traditional pearl bray boat duck cloth different colors. Canvas duck was the predominant awning fabric, a strong, closely woven cotton cloth used for centuries to make tents and sails.

The availability of different colors and stripes was the springboard for aesthetic uses of canvas awnings, which had previously been perceived as strictly utilitarian shading devices. The awning industry thrived from the post-Civil War period to after World War II.

On ornate examples, metal posts were adorned with filigree and the tops decorated with spear ends, balls or other embellishments. Iron plumbing pipe, which was quickly adapted for awning frames, became widely available and affordable as a result of mid-century industrialization. It was easily bent and threaded together to make a range of different shapes and sizes. Later, the introduction of retractable awnings meant that homeowners could adjust the awning easily and quickly to adapt to weather conditions. And, awnings can help save lives, just like in the movies: In 1933, a man in New York survived after his seven-story fall was slowed by several window awnings.

By the late 1940s, the new construction boom meant that newly built houses included air-conditioning, at the same time that more durable aluminum awnings gained in popularity. Older homes either removed their canvas awnings or replaced them with metal canopies by the 1950s.

OPPOSITE PAGE *Awnings provided shade and cooler air in an era that predated air-conditioning.*

LEFT *Many Charles Village homes were decorated with canvas window awnings.*

Rennert Hotel RAZED 1941

The Rennert Hotel was built in 1885 on the southwest corner of Liberty and Saratoga (Clay) Streets to the designs of architect E. F. Baldwin. An immediate success, the imposing brick and brownstone structure was expanded significantly as early as 1893. It was the flagship hotel in Robert Rennert's hotel business, having replaced two earlier hotels he built in Fayette Street. It quickly became known as the "Palace of the South," and was billed as the second-costliest edifice in the city.

The hotel was known nationally as a preferred meeting spot for politicians, who enjoyed the renowned southern-style seafood and raw oyster bar, an emerging and extravagant delicacy of the day. Writer H.L. Mencken could often be found in its main dining room, mingling with the city's elite. The hotel's registers from 1895 to 1920 are now housed at the Maryland Historical Society, and are a virtual who's who of the leading political figures of the day.

An all-black staff of cooks created masterpieces of entrées from local Maryland fish and fowl, with a menu listing a "tureen of butter-rich diamondback terrapin, a plump canvasback duck, and bulbous, briny oysters." Live Chesapeake terrapin were kept in cages in the basement, and joined pheasant, grouse, reed birds, hominy croquets and Maryland beaten biscuits on each luxurious menu.

Poet and anthologist Louis Untermeyer declared the Rennert home to be "the best restaurant in America" in his 1939 autobiography *From Another World*. If he had the choice of choosing the location of his death, he wrote that it would be "in the basement lunch-counter of the old Hotel Rennert . . . eating shad-roe and listening to Mencken with one ear and [the opera] *Die Meistersinger* with the other." In 1904, anxious hotel employees watched the Great Fire approach to within a block of the tall hotel.

The passage of Prohibition in 1919 eventually led to the downtown hotel falling behind on its property taxes, and while it slowly endured the Great Depression, the hostelry fell into receivership in 1932. It did appear that with the repeal of Prohibition in 1933 that the hotel would again flourish, with a famous picture of Mencken at the Rennert's mahogany bar, enjoying his first legal beer to much fanfare. However, the old style architecture and an aging infrastructure were demonstrated with the collapse of the dining room ceiling during a drunken fraternity dance in 1934. The Rennert closed its doors for good in 1939.

The hotel was demolished in 1941 and replaced with a parking garage nine years later. The garage was subsequently demolished in 1996, and is today surrounded by brown brick high-rise apartment complexes.

Robert Rennert also knew that his patrons tended to escape the summer heat in Baltimore, and so he built a summer resort coined Buena Vista in western Maryland northwest of Emmitsburg. (The hotel is shown above in the distance of this c. 1905 photo.) The wood frame main building was lined with porches on all levels, and a favorite destination of both Washingtonians and Baltimoreans of the day. It had its own railroad station and was referred to in newspapers as "the ambassadorial summer resort of the United States." The summer resort witnessed a similar fate as its urban counterpart, and was sold at auction in 1930 by Baltimore auctioneer Sam W. Pattison in 1930 for just $25,000 at the beginning of the Great Depression. The purchaser was the Jesuit order of St. Ignatius, who renamed it Bellarmine Hall. It housed priests and seminarians from Woodstock College, located nearby in the Patapsco River Valley. It was also used for religious retreats and day trips for the order's local educational institutions, Loyola High School and Loyola College. A modern complex replaced the original hotel, although several original outbuildings remain.

LEFT *The brick and brownstone Rennert Hotel was billed as the "Palace of the South."*

OPPOSITE PAGE *Politicians and well-known residents were drawn to the hotel's fine dining.*

St. Francis Xavier's Downtown Church

RAZED 1941

Baltimore has the distinction of having the first Roman Catholic Seminary in the United States (St. Mary's College and Seminary) and America's First Cathedral (the Baltimore Basilica). Baltimore can also tout that it had the first black Catholic Church in the United States and the first black Catholic priest ordained in the United States.

St. Francis Xavier Church was established in 1864 for black San Domingo refugees and the Sulpician Fathers, who had fled the French Revolution and settled in Baltimore, according to Agnes Kane Callum, historian for St. Francis Xavier Church. The Haitian refuges were among the 53 vessels that arrived in the Fell's Point neighborhood of Baltimore in 1793 escaping the revolution back home. The Catholic Haitians began attending Mass at St. Mary's Seminary in the basement, while also receiving education from the Catholic Church. They would later attend services at St. Ignatius Church on North Calvert Street.

In 1863, the First Universalist Church at the corner of Calvert and Pleasant Streets was purchased. The First Universalist Church was notable as it was the site of the Whig Party's political convention in 1844 when it nominated Henry Clay for president; four years later in 1848, the church was the site of the Democratic National Convention when Lewis Cass was nominated for president.

The large granite building—designed by famed Baltimore architect George A. Frederick, who also built Baltimore's City Hall—featured dramatic oval shaped side windows and was built in 1837. On February 21, 1864, one year after purchase, St. Francis Xavier Church was dedicated. Father Michael O'Connor was the church's first pastor.

According to the church, in 1871, four priests and Cardinal Herbert Vaughn arrived from Mill Hill, England, and were assigned as missionaries for the new church. These missionaries were sent to minister to black Catholics in Maryland, estimated to be more than 15,000 at the time. St. Francis Xavier Church soon saw a significant increase in attendance with three Masses each Sunday. Church historian Callum adds, "A priest house was opened and completely furnished on Courtland Street. A home for the aged poor was started and

an orphanage was operated. A night school was opened for adults; an industrial school was held in the basement of the church; and a lending library was held in the priest house."

"The Society of St. Joseph of the Sacred Heart of Jesus," known as the Josephite Fathers, was created in 1894. Three years prior, Baltimore again

had made history when Rev. Charles Randolph Uncles, S.S.J., was ordained as the first black Catholic priest in the United States. Uncles was ordained December 20, 1891. Uncles, whose father was a machinist with the Baltimore & Ohio Railroad, had been baptized in 1875 and confirmed in 1878, both at St. Francis Xavier Church. During this time, he was a printer and journalist, and later would teach at St. Francis Xavier's parish school and teach Latin and French at Epiphany College, the preparatory school for St. Joseph's Seminary in Baltimore. In 1880, Uncles became a teacher in Baltimore County; however, he soon left for Quebec, Canada to study theology. He returned to Baltimore in 1888 to enter St. Joseph's Seminary. In 1891, he was ordained as the first black Catholic priest in the United States.

St. Francis Xavier Church moved from its location at Calvert and Pleasant Streets in 1932, and one year later, Rev. Uncles died. St. Francis Xavier Church moved to a church at Eager and Caroline Streets before finally settling in East Baltimore in 1968 at Caroline and Oliver Streets.

The church's location at Calvert and Pleasant Streets was demolished in 1941 for a commercial building.

RIGHT *The original church at Calvert and Pleasant Streets. St. Francis Xavier Church was the first Catholic church in the country established for African-Americans.*

LEFT *The current St. Francis Xavier Church at Caroline and Oliver Streets.*

Centennial Fountain COLLAPSED 1945

Long before the Baltimore neighborhood was known as Bolton Hill, beginning in 1835, this area at the edge of the city was populated by several large mansions with expansive grounds. A land speculator named Edward Tiffany purchased the Gibson Mansion in 1850, along with its 15 acres of landscaped grounds. He petitioned and gained approval to create a grand and wide boulevard to be called Eutaw Place between the 1200 and 1500 blocks, with a series of garden squares.

Tiffany's intention was not to beautify his own land, but to lay out a tree lined street where he could build speculative townhouses on individual lots, hoping to lure new homeowners desiring to mingle with the city's most wealthy citizens. The former mansions known as Rose Hill, Bolton, and Mount Royal soon gave way to elegant streets lined with large townhouses found in the neighborhood today.

At the confluence of Eutaw Place and McMechen Street, a large fountain was installed in 1877 that became known as the Centennial Fountain. Previously known as the Children's Fountain, it was renamed because it had first been installed at the country's Centennial Exposition in Philadelphia in 1876. It was purchased from Mott & Company of New York by residents of Eutaw Place for a mere $9,000, a fraction of its original cost to construct.

By the 1880s, the streets surrounding the newly installed fountain were home to various members of the wealthy German-Jewish community with notable names such as Hecht, Hutzler, Bragers, Strouse, and Hochchild, who owned department stores, clothing manufacturing, and dry-goods businesses.

The massive fountain was officially turned on May 19, 1877. As described by historian John Thomas Scharf (1843–98):

The outer basin is 48 feet in diameter, and the main fountain, standing upon a granite base, is 50 feet high and has three distinct basins, the water flowing from the two upper ones to the lower, which is 10 feet in diameter and richly ornamented. A graceful female figure, standing in a shell, surmounts the work. Smaller figures on the surface of the water, and vases of flowers surrounding the outer basin, complete one of the most beautiful fountains in the city.

Long thought dismantled for scrap during World War II, the Centennial Fountain actually collapsed

under the weight of ice and snow in 1945. The removal of the adjacent benches was called "an indecency" by neighbors.

Following a period of severe decline of the neighborhood in the 1960s and 1970s, the homes lining Eutaw Place were eventually restored during the next two decades. The Bolton Hill Garden Club was able to retrieve and restore a fountain in the 1800 block of Eutaw Place in 2009. The fountain had once been located on the grounds of a nursing home in downtown Baltimore, but eventually ended up in storage in the Odorite Building. When that building was razed, the fountain was sadly chained to a fence in a parking lot.

Members of the Bolton Hill Garden Club and the Mid-Town Community Benefits organization agreed to raise funds and install the replacement fountain, which was unveiled in 2009.

ABOVE *Bolton Hill has been home to several other prominent fountains, including this, the Gunther Fountain.*

OPPOSITE PAGE AND LEFT *Centennial Fountain, built in 1877, contributed to the bucolic nature of Bolton Hill.*

Calvert Street Station RAZED 1948

The Calvert Street Station officially opened in 1850 as the city's southern terminus for the Baltimore and Susquehanna Railroad (B&S). Following a two-year construction period, the building consolidated both passenger and freight traffic for the railroad. The B&S line had operated since 1829; however, a track was built to Lake Roland, and shortly thereafter was extended to Cockeysville, Maryland.

The new city station was designed in an Italianate style by J. Crawford Neilson of the architectural firm of Niernsee and Neilson, and constructed of brown freestone that had been quarried along the railroad lines. It was located at North Calvert and Franklin Streets, on the site of a massive Roman Amphitheater that had been built for outside performances in 1846, but tragically burned to the ground just a year later.

The 1850 *American Railroad Journal* stated that "the depot, for spaciousness, convenience, and adaptation to the purpose for which it is designed, will compare most favorably in every respect with any in the United States." The local *Baltimore Clipper* newspaper covered the opening on June 4, 1850, noting that a large number of spectators met the arrival of the first train to use the building.

OPPOSITE PAGE *The Italianate style building served both passenger and freight traffic.*
BELOW *A 1936 photograph of Calvert Station's north end train shed.*

The station and railroad was successful for a number of decades, ferrying thousands of passengers to and from a string of small towns in the region. A grand reception for the Prince of Wales was held at the station for his arrival in 1860; he would later be crowned King Edward VII. During the Civil War, the station served as the starting point for shipments to the battle of Gettysburg, and served as a hospital relief center afterwards.

The B&S had consolidated into the Pennsylvania Railroad in 1854, which in turn became the Northern Central Railroad in 1875. As late as World War II, the Northern Central hosted 34 passenger trains among three different branches serving destinations as far off as Buffalo, New York and Cleveland, Ohio. In Baltimore City, the commuter line was known as Parkton Local and the Baltimore-Harrisburg Local. Stops included Woodbury, Cylburn, Ruxton, Lutherville, Timonium, and Cockeysville.

With improved roads, highways, and more and more families buying multiple automobiles, the passenger traffic at Calvert Street Station steadily declined. The building was razed in 1948 to make way for the current headquarters of the *Baltimore Sun*.

THE PLOT THICKENS

The Baltimore Plot was an alleged conspiracy in February of 1861 to assassinate President-elect Abraham Lincoln at the Calvert Street Station, where he was scheduled to change trains. Allan Pinkerton was in charge of protecting Lincoln during his whistle stop tour of 70 towns and cities that ended with his inauguration in Washington, D.C. Historians continue to debate if the assassination attempt was ever a real threat, however. Pinkerton became convinced that a plot existed to ambush Lincoln's carriage between the Calvert Street

Station of the Northern Central Railway and the Camden Street Station of the Baltimore and Ohio Railroad. Lincoln would change trains in Baltimore on February 23, 1861. He tried to persuade Lincoln to cancel his stop at Harrisburg, Pennsylvania, and to precede secretly straight through Baltimore, but Lincoln insisted upon keeping to his schedule. He passed through Baltimore in the middle of the night. After Lincoln was safely on the train to Washington, D.C., Pinkerton sent a one-line telegram to the president of the Philadelphia, Wilmington and Baltimore Railroad that read: "Plums delivered nuts safely." Lincoln's many critics would hound him for the cowardly act of sneaking through Baltimore at night, allegedly in disguise, sacrificing his honor for his personal safety.

Old Lexington Market BURNED 1949

Billed as "The World's Largest, Continuously Running Market," Lexington Market has been a stalwart destination for food shopping and dining in Baltimore for over 200 years. Dating back to 1782 on Lexington Street in downtown Baltimore, the land was donated by General John Eager Howard. Original vendors sold meats, produce, and dairy goods from their horse-drawn wagons, followed by a wooden shed in 1803. Eventually a more organized market was constructed, originally called the "Western Precinct Market," until its name was changed to Lexington Market in 1818.

Lexington Market would soon become world famous, visited by politicians, artists, and even world-known writers such as Ralph Waldo Emerson, who when he visited Lexington Market proclaimed Baltimore as the "Gastronomical Center of the Universe." As the nation's second largest city in the 1830s and 1850s, Lexington Market became not just a market destination for Baltimoreans but those along the East Coast as well.

By the early 20th century, there were over 1,000 stalls, and like many markets today, certain areas were designated for different types of food—meats, fish, cheese, etc. With its growth, Lexington Market also faced increased opposition from politicians and community leaders who saw the market's increased traffic as a nuisance.

On March 29, 1949, however, a six-alarm broke out in Lexington Market, destroying most of the market. Luckily, a new brick and glass market was constructed at the same location, incorporating improvements for parking, air conditioning, and sanitary conditions, and the new Lexington Market opened in April 1952. Baltimore City added a two-story, 20,000-square-foot addition in 1982, and in 2001, as part of Baltimore's West Side Renaissance Plan, Lexington Market received $3 million in renovation funding.

Today, Lexington Market continues to sell fresh produce, meats, seafood, and baked goods, as well as general merchandise, gifts, prepared foods and restaurants, including Faidley's Seafood, world-known for its crab cakes.

And although large supermarkets, as well as discount stores like Target and Wal-mart, have moved into Baltimore City with increased regularity, offering residents increased options for grocery shopping, local markets and farmers' markets continue to thrive in Baltimore. Cross Street Market in Federal Hill is still a popular shopping destination for South Baltimore residents, which is especially vital in an area that does not have ample access to large grocery stores. Cross Street Market's vendors include meat, seafood and produce sellers, as well as an array of carry-out food stalls and floral shops, and the market has tapped into a younger market by opening its doors on weekend nights, offering beer and food for sale.

Other areas of Baltimore City also still have viable markets—Broadway Market in Fell's Point, Hollins Market near the University of Maryland's medical campus, among others—as well as successful farmers' markets that dot the city, including the year-round Waverly Farmers' Market and the Baltimore Farmers' Market located under the JFX downtown. Especially for those residents without access to cars, these markets, as well as the historic Lexington Market, still fill a critical need.

OPPOSITE PAGE *This 1905 image shows one of the market's fruit stalls on the corner of West Lexington and West Eutaw streets.*

BELOW *Horse-drawn wagons brought fresh produce to Lexington Market.*

FOLLOWING PAGE *An elevated view of Lexington Market from 1903. By this time, the market had more than 1,000 stalls.*

Fruit and Seafood Industry WANED 1950s

Baltimore is known globally for its seafood industry, most especially crabs, as tourists from all over the world come to Baltimore to taste Maryland crab cakes. However, in the late 1800s and early 1900s, oysters, watermelons and bananas were the most common foods coming into Baltimore. Due to its proximity to the seafood-rich Chesapeake Bay and the agriculturally based Eastern Shore, Baltimore was a natural port on entry for both oysters and fruit. Plus, Baltimore had a sophisticated railroad system, allowing items to be quickly unloaded from ships and immediately loaded onto adjacent rail cars.

One of the biggest crops into Baltimore was the arrival of watermelons. Twice a week shipments of the summer treat arrived into Baltimore, and the news of their arrival was covered extensively in local newspapers. An August 1892 article in the *Baltimore Sun* documented the watermelon shipment into Baltimore from farms in Anne Arundel, Caroline, Dorchester and Wicomico Counties. It estimated that 8,000 watermelons and 10,000 cantaloupes were consumed each day in Baltimore, and that 25,000 watermelons arrived each week in Baltimore.

They are shipped in vessels of every description – schooners, bug eyes, sloops and canoes. On arriving in Baltimore the cargoes are put in the hands of commission merchants who dispose of them to retail dealers and out of town shippers. The smaller dealers load wagons, travel through the streets and yell at the top of their not altogether musical voices the magic names of their wares. The bulk of the crop is purchased by out of town shippers who load the melons on cars and ship them to other States, where the Maryland watermelon is considered a necessity in summer.

Baltimore was also a major port for the banana industry and was called "The First Big Banana Port" with 35,000 bunches of bananas arriving on some days. One of the biggest banana importers was the United Fruit Company.

The fruit industry did suffer a major blow in 1937 at the Jackson Wharf Freight Station in Fell's Point where three finger piers had been constructed in 1872 for schooners to unload watermelons. On February 10, 1937, one of the finger piers fell into the harbor carrying two men into the water and seven boxcars. It was never replaced.

In addition to watermelons and bananas, Baltimore has also been a major port for the oyster industry. Its easy access to the Chesapeake Bay—the name Chesapeake comes from the Algonquin word "Chesipiook," which translates to "Great Shellfish Bay"—made Baltimore a natural port of entry. The brackish waters of the Chesapeake provide the perfect environment for oysters to thrive, and as early as 1836, Baltimore had an oyster canning facility.

Oyster production peaked in the mid-1880s with around 14 million bushels of oysters harvested from the Chesapeake Bay, which employed 20 percent of fishery workers in the entire country. One downside of the burst of oyster canning in Baltimore was the use of child labor. As late as 1889, laws allowed children 10 years of age to work in the manufacturing sector for 10 hours a day, although future laws raised the age limits and reduced the number of hours. However, canneries were many times exempt from child labor laws, and as late as 1915, students under the age of 16 were still allowed to work in the canneries during school hours if their local school would vouch that they could read and write.

LEFT *Bananas arriving in 1905. Note evidence in the background of the previous year's Great Baltimore Fire.*

RIGHT *Merchants unload oyster luggers in Baltimore. Oysters were a major product in the late 1800s.*

Light Street Wharves GONE 1950s

Motorists traversing on Light Street by Pratt Street today face bumper-to-bumper traffic almost daily. Likewise, in the mid- to late 1800s and early 1900s, the Light Street/Pratt Street corridor was equally congested due to the Light Street Wharves, a collection of warehouse-type buildings where steamers and other vessels docked and cargo was loaded on and off.

The Light Street Wharves and the adjacent tobacco warehouses on East Conway Street created a bustling area downtown. Light Street was a narrow thoroughfare with horse-drawn wagons, and the street level piers blocked the view of the Harbor from downtown. After the Great Baltimore Fire of 1904, Light Street was widened beginning in 1907 to allow for greater traffic flow.

Businesses also sprang up around the piers, servicing dockworkers and employees of the steamships. Barber shops, cafes and, most commonly, saloons dotted the area.

Although the Light Street Wharf area was bustling, it did suffer its share of hardship. In 1921, frigid temperatures resulted in an Ice Embargo as waters were frozen all the way to the York River, resulting in a huge financial loss for the city and the steamship companies. "[Light] Street, which, under ordinary conditions, presents a spectacle of congested traffic, is now practically deserted. No longer is the lusty shout of the stevedores heard. Instead the boats are lying quietly tied up at their moorings, with thin columns of smoke hanging over their stacks," the *Baltimore Sun* reported.

Later that year, with the arrival of spring it was reported that activity was back to its hectic pace with commodities of every kind being shipped—beds, chairs, stacks of fertilizer, baled cotton, chicken crates, lawn swings—all going to farms on the Eastern and Western Shores of Maryland.

Mother Nature dealt the Light Street Wharves another blow in 1933. The Chesapeake-Potomac Hurricane hit Baltimore, flooding the Light Street Wharves. Light Street was described as a "veritable sea" by the *Baltimore Sun*.

During World War II, the Light Street Wharves were very active (smoking was also banned due to fears of fire on ships carrying war cargo), but by the end of the war, many were hardly used. In 1944, the mayor suggested converting the wharves into a waterfront park. The wharves were in poor shape and considered by many to be a fire hazard and an eyesore. In 1948, a plan was proposed asking for voters to approve a $1.5 million bond to allow the acquisition of all the properties along the east side of Light Street, the construction of new wharves and warehouses, and new traffic patterns to relieve congestion on Light Street.

In 1950, the wharves were razed and Sam Smith Park was built. The park was later built over for the construction of Harborplace in 1980, which would fuel the revitalization of Baltimore's Inner Harbor.

ABOVE *A variety of merchants lined the busy wharf area.*

LEFT *Eventually, the wharves fell into disrepair and were razed in the 1950s.*

RIGHT *The imposing buildings along Light Street blocked the water views for residents.*

FOLLOWING PAGE *Light Street was a bustling thoroughfare in the early 20th century.*

Historic Homes of Fell's Point GONE LATE 1950s

The scenic waterfront neighborhood of Fell's Point contains some of Baltimore's oldest homes and iconic features such as stone streets, haunted watering holes, and beautiful waterfront views. The neighborhood has done an outstanding job of preserving the historic homes, but like any centuries-old neighborhood, some old homes have been razed due to commercial growth and neglect.

Fell's Point was founded by William Fell in 1730 when he bought a 100-acre tract of land and set up a small shipbuilding operation. William Fell built a

mansion for his family, and named his tract of land, "Fell's Prospect." His son, Edward, later laid out streets in 1763 and named the neighborhood "Fell's Point." Edward, who had also inherited a large amount of land from his Uncle Edward, sold some of the acreage in lots for people to build homes. Lot 65 contained 1621 Thames Street and was in possession by the Fell family. There is much debate whether the home at 1621 was lived in by William Fell, founder of the neighborhood, but most evidence points to the fact that the estimated

OPPOSITE PAGE *The double wide home at 520–522 South Chapel Street was considered one of the oldest buildings remaining in Baltimore until its demolition.*

BELOW *1621 Thames Street offered excellent water views.*

construction date falls after William's death in 1746. It is concluded that the home at 1621 Thames Street was owned by William's only son, Edward, who had married his cousin Ann Bond, the daughter of John Bond, a merchant and prominent citizen of Fell's Point.

When Edward died, however, it is presumed that he was living in his father's former house on Lancaster Street. The family burial plot is nearby on Shakespeare Street. Edward died at the age of 33 in 1766. His widow sold the home to her father John Bond, whose estate sold the home and various other neighborhood properties in 1798 to William Jackson for 3,000 pounds. Jackson sold 1621 Thames Street the same year, and eventually, it was owned by another prominent merchant named Robert Oliver. The home was sold many times, eventually acquired by default of mortgage in 1924, and bought by Associated Mortgages in 1936, also by default of mortgage.

The brick home with a wood shingle roof fell into deep disrepair and was abandoned after being used as a plumber's shop. The dilapidated home was vandalized and broken into, with many of the original interior features stolen.

Along with the neighboring homes, 1621–1637 Thames Street were all demolished to make way for

LEFT *It is clear from its opulent interior that 1621 Thames Street was home to prominent residents.*

LEFT BELOW *A grocery store at the corner of Thames Street and South Broadway in 1936.*

OPPOSITE PAGE *Many homes in the 1600 block of Thames Street were razed for a brick commercial building.*

WELL PRESERVED

Despite the loss of the homes featured here, Fell's Point has been one of the leading communities in historic preservation and a walk through the neighborhood today transports one back in time. Today's shops, restaurants, and commercial structures blend in with the old homes, as many are housed within 19th-century homes themselves. However, a 1960s highway plan would have destroyed much, if not all, of Fell's Point (as well as its waterfront neighbor Federal Hill, including the park), were it not for the grassroots efforts of some Fell's Point residents and The Society for Preservation of Federal Hill and Fell's Point, who took on the government and saved two historic neighborhoods. By the late 1960s, a plan was being proposed to extend two of Baltimore's interstates, I-95 and I-83. When word of this got out, some Fell's Point businesses closed and it was a foregone conclusion that the highways would be constructed; however, the residents of Fell's Point refused to lie down. The 1969 "Baltimore 3-A Interstate and Boulevard System" plan would have extended I-83 south and east through Fell's Point on a six-lane elevated viaduct, before continuing east along Boston Street to junction I-95. In the mid-1970s, another plan was proposed that would have I-83 continue south and descend into a six-lane underwater tunnel under the Inner Harbor, turn east and past Fell's Point before

a brick retail center. Today, 1621 Thames Street is home to a shop called 10,000 Villages, a fair trade retailer selling wares from around the world. The historic double home at 520–522 South Chapel Street in Fell's Point has also been razed. South Chapel Street was originally called Star Alley. The double home at 520–522 South Chapel Street was a modest one, and the roof was raised at the rear to expand the home's height. Before demolition, 520–522 South Chapel Street was considered one of the oldest homes remaining in Fell's Point. It was razed sometime after 1936.

resurfacing to join I-95. Neither plan came to fruition. Upon hearing of the original plan, the Preservation Society began raising awareness through walking tours and events to show the citizenry the importance of preserving the oldest waterfront community in Baltimore. In April 1969, 23 residents filed a lawsuit claiming that many buildings had been declared historic sites of local, state, and national significance. To help fund the legal costs, the Preservation Society held many events that are still celebrated today. The largest one—the Fell's Point Fun Festival—began in 1966 to help fund the effort to halt the highway construction. The event is held each October and draws over 700,000 visitors. A Harbor Ball was held in 1970, and a Historic Harbor House Tour followed. One of the key advocates was Councilwoman Barbara Mikulski (now a U.S. Senator and the longest serving woman in the history of Congress), who introduced several anti-highway bills during the contentious fight that dragged on for several years. The Preservation Society led the effort to have both communities listed on the National Register of Historic Places. Fell's Point became a National Register Historic District in 1969 (making it the second historic district in the United States to receive that honor) and Federal Hill a year later. The highway project was successfully thwarted and the neighborhoods preserved.

019127. HOTEL KERNAN & MARYL
BALTIMORE, MD.

Downtown Theaters GONE 1960s

In the early 20th century, Baltimore was home to a number of elegant theatres, most especially in the downtown area near Howard Street, which also contained antique shops and grand hotels.

While the Front Street Theatre, built in 1829, was important historically (it was the scene of the presidential nominations of both Stephen A. Douglas and Abraham Lincoln), it was in the early 20th century when the beautiful and elaborately decorated theaters began to pop up in downtown Baltimore. The Maryland Theatre was built by James Kernan in 1903 and would serve as the debut location for Al Jolson. Kernan had previously owned the Monumental Theatre, which focused on more daring, sensual acts, but with his second theater, the Maryland Theatre, Kernan featured more family friendly vaudeville acts, including animal acts and acrobatics. The adjacent Kernan

OPPOSITE PAGE *The Kernan Hotel (right) remains today; however, the Maryland Theatre (left) was demolished in 1951.*

BELOW *The Gayety was home to famous comedians, but most notably to burlesque acts.*

Hotel was equally elegant as the theater. Eventually, the Maryland Theatre, like many others in the city, focused more on motion pictures. It was demolished in 1951.

Known by several names—the Holliday Street Theatre, the Old Drury, the New Theatre, among others—the New Theater on Holliday Street is perhaps most famous for being the venue that first performed Francis Scott-Key's "Star-Spangled Banner." The elegantly designed theater first opened in 1795 and featured acts ranging from opera to comedy to dance. Later, in 1813, a new brick building replaced the original structure. John T. Ford would later purchase the historic theater. Ford also owned the Ford Theatre and Ford's Opera House in Baltimore, as well as the famous Ford Theatre in Washington, D.C., site of the assassination of President Abraham Lincoln. He would manage the New Theatre on Holliday Street in Baltimore for over 20 years, which he rebuilt after an 1873 fire. It would later showcase motion pictures before it was razed in 1917. The War Memorial Plaza stands where the theater once was.

The Ford Theatre in Baltimore, meanwhile, was the site of the 1872 Democratic National Convention, in addition to being a venue for musical acts. Before its closure, it was the scene of protests by the National Association for the Advancement of Colored People (NAACP) for its segregation policy. Blacks were able to purchase tickets for movies shown there but were relegated to the balcony areas. It was razed in the 1960s, as was the Stanley Theatre.

While most of the classic theaters were centered around the Howard Street area, another separate theater district existed on Pennsylvania Avenue in Baltimore. Home to entertainment venues for Baltimore's black community (Baltimore was still a rather segregated city), Pennsylvania Avenue was home to the Royal Theatre, originally called the Douglas Theatre. Some of the biggest names in music played at the Royal, including Al Jolson, Cab Calloway, Billie Holiday, Ella Fitzgerald, Nat King Cole, James Brown, and The Supremes. It later would show movies until it was razed to make way for a school.

Baltimore was also home to some theaters that focused on more sensational acts. The Lyceum opened in the late 19th century and showed musical and vaudeville acts, but was perhaps best known for the risqué acts it featured before it burned down in 1925. Additionally, Baltimore Street (now known as "The Block" and home to several strip clubs) contained many burlesque clubs, most famously the Gayety Theatre.

The Gayety, owned by John Nickel beginning in 1910, featured famous comedians such as Jackie Gleason and Abbott and Costello, but it was best known for talents such as Gypsy Rose Lee, Margie Hart, Ann Corio, and Blaze Starr, a Baltimore native. The Gayety was patronized by locals, as well as soldiers during World War II and politicians. The Gayety was wildly successful with shows lasting over two hours featuring comedians, singers, and burlesque. Later, Nickel's two children operated the Gayety. Today, it is home to an adult store and the Hustler Club.

LEFT *The Lyric Theatre (now the Lyric Opera House) was built in 1894. Following extensive renovations in the early 1980s, it is now unrecognizable from its former self.*

RIGHT *The once vibrant theater district on Baltimore's West Side is now a neighborhood looking to rebound. This photo includes the Maryland Theatre, far left, and the Auditorium Theatre and Academy of Music on the right.*

Marble Step Cleaning **WANED 1960s**

Baltimore has many societal traditions— enthusiastic passion for its sports teams like the Ravens and Orioles, obsession with crabs, as well as some quirkier nuances such as the use of the word "Hon" as a friendly greeting, beehive hairdos, and interesting pronunciations of words such as "Balamer" and "Merlin" for the name of its city and state. One Baltimore tradition that may not be completely gone but has waned over the past 50 years and even when practiced is done in a less structured way is the cleaning of the front marble steps.

White marble graces the front steps of thousands of Baltimore row houses. Many feature marble from Cockeysville, a Baltimore suburb, as the town's quarries supplied marble used on the Washington Monument in Washington, D.C., the Washington Monument in downtown Baltimore, and the National Capitol in Washington, D.C. In addition to these iconic monuments, white marble was also used to build the front steps leading up to Baltimore row houses in many neighborhoods, including Fell's Point, Canton, Federal Hill, Bolton Hill, as well as working-class neighborhoods in Southwest Baltimore.

White marble was used not only for its available access in nearby Cockeysville, but also for its durable nature and its sharp contrast to the red brick that graced many row houses.

Baltimoreans took pride in their white marble steps, and the front stoop became a focal gathering point for neighbors to talk to each other before the days of fenced-in back yards. Even today, Baltimoreans are known for "sitting on the front stoop," especially on cool evenings, and during the summer for those homes without central air conditioning. Neighborhood groups also urged residents to sit on the front stoop to help reduce crime and look after each other.

Although the white marble steps were attractive, the porous nature of marble also allowed everyday dirt from people's shoes, as well as smoke and pollution from city life, to penetrate the marble steps, resulting in an unsightly appearance.

In the early to mid-20th century, a weekly ritual for many Baltimore housewives was the scrubbing and cleaning of the front marble steps. Used as a way to show pride of homeownership as well as a way to visit with neighbors, women would scrub the steps, usually on Saturdays, until they gleamed. Many different cleaning products were used, but most women used Bon Ami powder and warm water and used a metal bristle brush or pumice stone. Even today, local shops sell a kit that includes Bon Ami and a pumice stone. Bon Ami, headquartered in Kansas City, Missouri and featuring the tagline, "Hasn't Scratched Yet" and an adorable baby chicken in their advertisements, is still in business after 125 years.

Homeowners would urge others to "Keep Off the Steps" to protect the shiny white marble. Today, there are neighborhood activists and artists who are trying to bring back this ritual of cleaning the white marble steps regularly to improve home value, bond with neighbors, and develop a camaraderie as a neighborhood. However, what was once a weekly ritual for housewives in Baltimore has waned over the years due to busier lives, the increase of women working outside the home, and changing priorities.

BELOW AND RIGHT *Baltimore housewives, and sometimes their daughters, took pride in their white marble steps. Scrubbing them clean was a weekly ritual.*

Cast Iron Bridges REMOVED 1960s

Many people associate buildings and bridges constructed with cast iron as a product of the Industrial Revolution. The use of cast iron is much older, however, with the first cast iron arch bridge being built over the River Severn in Shropshire, England in 1779. The material was previously too expensive for use in building large structures.

Baltimore was in the forefront of utilizing cast iron in both buildings and bridges by the mid 19th century. Created by pouring melted pig iron into often elaborately decorated molds, the molten material could be manipulated for use in everything from architectural trim work to vital support columns. Generally brittle, cast iron is weak under tension yet very strong under compression. Its load-bearing qualities are greater than brick while obviously using less space. Notable foundries located in Baltimore meant that the material was in abundance and relatively inexpensive. They included Hayward, Bartlett & Company, and the Poole-Hunt Foundry.

Railroads had been dealing for decades with wooden bridges that were susceptible to collapse and fire, both of which happened frequently. The first iron truss bridge designed and built in the United States was developed by Baltimore native Wendel Bollman (1814–84). A self-taught engineer,

Bollman had begun work laying railroad track at age 15. Working under the son of renowned architect of the U.S. Capitol building Benjamin Henry Latrobe, Jr., in 1847, Bollman was named head of the Baltimore & Ohio Railroad bridges along the Harper Ferry line.

A few years later, his newly designed span had refined previous versions that were susceptible to collapse under the strain of heavy locomotives, and his iron truss bridge was quickly adopted by the railroad as a standard. He wisely received a patent for his design. He was noted for implementing math and logic and was instrumental in approaching civil engineering with a scientific approach. Bollman was named Master of Roads for the B&O in 1851; he built a total of 12 bridges in Baltimore, and witnessed his design constructed as far away as China.

Railroad bridges were not the only spans constructed of cast iron. With the Jones Falls winding its way throughout the city, hundreds of pedestrian and commercial bridges were needed to span the ravine. Perhaps one of the more aesthetic paired spans was built on St. Paul Street over Jones Falls at Union (now Pennsylvania) Railroad Station. Adjacent to the formal Mount Royal Terrace Gardens, and constructed in the 1870s, the

southernmost span featured two female sculptures by D. A. Henning that represented truth and justice.

Designed in 1877 by engineer Wendel Bollman, the Lombard Street Bridge was a unique, bifurcated watermain, which is an integral part in the support system for the bridge. It was built to carry both traffic over the Jones Falls as well as water pumped through the large arched pipe. The bridge was disassembled about 1975 due to concerns about increasingly heavy traffic on Lombard Street, and is currently stored in pieces at the Baltimore Streetcar Museum.

Generally, the use of cast iron on bridges and architecture fell out of fashion with architects beginning in the late 1800s with the advent of inexpensively produced steel. The increasing automobile traffic called for new, wider bridges to be built of concrete. Sadly, only one Bollman bridge remains today, located in Savage, Maryland. His Harper's Ferry bridge was removed several times during the Civil War, but was rebuilt and lasted until 1936, when it was destroyed during a major flood.

ABOVE *The Lombard Street Bridge was built for both traffic and as a water main over the Jones Falls.*

LEFT *This trust bridge, built in 1886, crossed Lake Roland.*

OPPOSITE PAGE *The dramatic bridge on St. Paul Street ran alongside Penn Station.*

Baltimore City Jail PARTIALLY RAZED 1961

The plight of the Baltimore City Jail, located near downtown and visible from I-83 has a long and complicated history, most of it involving political blunders and the old opposition saying, "Not in My Back Yard."

The first Baltimore City Jail was constructed in 1801 at Buren and East Madison Streets, site of today's jail. In 1855, the Baltimore City Council concluded that a new jail was necessary and solicited design plans by architects. The following year, work was to begin with the brother architectural team of Thomas and James Dixon, well-known architects of several prominent churches in Baltimore. However, some commissioners wanted to modify the plans to allow for larger cells, improved ventilation, and quarters for the warden. The City Commissioner, Joseph P. Shannon commissioned a more extravagant design from the architect Gridley Bryant. However, Bryant's design proved too costly, Shannon was dismissed from his position, and the Dixon team resumed their original design beginning in 1857.

The Dixons' design was a beautiful Gothic structure, a large rectangular building with a central block and two long wings. Built on the "Auburn Plan," creating a "prison within a prison," it was over 400 feet in length and constructed of stone, brick, and iron. It was regarded as a distinguished example of mid-19th century prison architecture upon its completion in 1859.

Inside, two cell blocks were each composed of five stories of 30 cells each for a total of 300 cells. In 1905, the cell block wings were extended 50 feet.

Over the years, however, the prison population started to outgrow the old Gothic prison. In 1952, a study was conducted to examine the state of the current jail. The almost century-old prison was starting to show its age, and by 1952, it was housing 25 percent more than its capacity of 800 prisoners. Also of concern were the original 1859 locks that had to be locked and unlocked individually, a concern in the case of fire. A new building was also proposed to allow for the separation of juveniles; at the time of the study, there were 17 juveniles under age 16 housed at the City Jail.

The same year as the study, voters approved a $6 million bond to erect a new jail. A new Baltimore City Jail Commission recommended to Mayor Thomas D'Alesandro that the jail be constructed on the grounds of the City Hospital in East Baltimore. The following year, the Commission reiterated its position as no progress had been made. Residents of the surrounding East Baltimore neighborhoods aggressively protested against the new jail site, not wanting to live near a facility housing violent criminals. Other sites were considered, including Harbor Field (former home of Baltimore Municipal Airport), Fort Carroll, Herring Run Park, Loch Raven watershed, and the current jail site at Buren and Madison Streets. The Jail Commission rejected all of these sites and continued to recommend the City Hospital site for the new jail.

As plans for the new jail languished, the public grew restless and local newspapers blasted Mayor D'Alesandro for refusing to act and calling into question where the $6 million bond was. Finally, in 1956, the City purchased a tract of land owned by the Pennsylvania Railroad adjacent to the old jail. In 1959, a new maximum security prison began construction on the site of the old jail.

With the new prison construction underway, Baltimore City approved a plan to demolish the original walls, and remove all the Gothic revival architectural elements. Large portions of the old jail were razed, the pitched slate roof was eliminated, as well as the central octagonal cupola with Gothic tracery, and the white marble and granite Tudor watchtowers. In the new design, brick veneer would be utilized to mimic the new building. Preservationists pointed out that the old jail was only one of 13 Baltimore sites included in the Historic American Buildings Survey conducted by the Library of Congress, but the City concluded that the costs associated with preserving the original structure were too high.

In 1961, the first prisoners moved into the new jail. The Gatehouse at the Warden's residence is the only surviving exterior portion of the Tudor Gothic-inspired City Jail and remains as one of Baltimore's most picturesque, non-ecclesiastical Gothic structures.

LEFT *Much of the jail's original Gothic revival touches were removed in the 1950s and 1960s.*

OPPOSITE PAGE *Construction of the imposing Baltimore City Jail was completed in 1859.*

Baltimore Quarantine Station CLOSED 1961

Although New York's Ellis Island is the most well known immigration port in the United States, Baltimore was also a leading port of entry in the 19th and 20th centuries (see sidebar). Due to this, The City of Baltimore built a Quarantine Station near the Key Bridge, mainly in response to the yellow fever epidemic of 1794. The station was moved several times, finally settling in around 1881 at Leading Point on the west side of the Patapsco River, eight miles from Ft. McHenry. Like most quarantine stations in the United States (the National Quarantine Act of 1893 created a national system of quarantine while still permitting state-run quarantines), the Baltimore Quarantine Station was purposely situated far from heavily populated areas of the city. The U.S. Public Health Service took control of the Baltimore station in 1918,

Consisting of four buildings—a barracks for infected patients to receive medical attention, an officers' dormitory, storage facility, and a building for administration offices and beds for laborers—the station also contained a de-lousing plant.

As ships arrived, quarantine officers boarded to verify documentation outlining the number of officers, vessel description, crew and passengers aboard, and health records of the ship and its passengers. The ship's officers also had to inform the quarantine officers if any passengers had become ill or died during the passage and the reason for the illness or death. As a heavy point of entry, the Baltimore Quarantine Station faced a steady steam of ships on a daily basis.

Some of the contagious diseases that officers were most concerned with included yellow fever, smallpox, cholera, leprosy, and the plague. Those infected passengers (and many times the entire manifest of passengers, crew, and cargo for infected ships) were taken to the onsite hospital for treatment. In addition to infected ship passengers, the Baltimore Quarantine Station also took care of local Baltimore residents infected with smallpox. Immigrants into the United States were inspected at the Locust Point quarantine station at the immigration piers.

OPPOSITE PAGE *The Quarantine Station was located at Leading Point and allowed officers to inspect ships.*

BELOW *Thousands of immigrants were processed at the immigration station at Locust Point.*

SECOND ONLY TO ELLIS ISLAND

During the late 19th and early 20th centuries, Baltimore was the second leading port of entry for immigrants, only behind New York's Ellis Island. While Irish and German immigrants came in droves, some of the earliest immigrants were white and black refugees escaping a revolution in Haiti who arrived in 1793. Before the Civil War, immigrants arrived in Fell's Point's Henderson Wharf, primarily Germans and Irish. The rise in German immigrants was fueled by the trading links established between Baltimore and Bremen and its port of Bremerhaven, the leading port for the import of Maryland tobacco and the leading port of embarkation in Europe, with immigrants from all over Eastern Europe setting sail to the United States. By 1868, Locust Point was the epicenter of immigration into Baltimore. On March 24, 1868, the Baltimore & Ohio Railroad's Locust Point immigration piers opened to greet the German steamer, *Baltimore*, which carried passengers as well as German goods. It returned to Europe with Maryland tobacco and lumber. Interestingly, only steerage class passengers were required to undergo health and customs examinations. Many Germans who came through Locust Point settled in the neighborhood, and German influence is still felt today in the tight-knot neighborhood. Irish men, meanwhile, primarily worked for the B&O Railroad, while women worked as domestics. In 1913, the federal government built a three-building Locust Point Immigration Center to replace the B&O piers. However, the timing was unfortunate as once World War I broke out, immigration slowed. In fact, the new Immigration Center was never utilized and today serves as a Naval Reserve Training Center. In all, nearly two million immigrants landed in Baltimore, approximately one million at the B&O Railroad's Locust Point immigration piers.

Jones Falls COVERED BY JFX HIGHWAY 1962

Many commuters racing down the 19-mile long Jones Falls Expressway (JFX) today might wonder why the highway has rather dramatic and drastic curves as it leads drivers from the outer beltway to the Inner Harbor. That's because when it was planned in the 1950s, and built in the 1960s, it followed the path of a mostly placid stream called the Jones Falls. Only small bits of the stream can be seen today, mostly covered with concrete tunnels supporting the elevated highway.

Early in its history, the Jones Falls was an urban stream that was used for fishing and picnicking as it ran through the streets of Baltimore City. Local writer Letitia Stockett described it as "that belligerent little stream," but in fact it was prone to frequent flooding, and soon became an open sewer for a growing city. Beginning in 1815, the city built stone retaining walls in an attempt to control the flow of water, especially during periods of heavy rain.

As early as 1817, however, planner Benjamin Latrobe proposed covering the falls all together, as would countless other urban planners in the decades to come. A major wall construction project commenced following the devastating flood of 1868. Jones Falls was credited in stopping the raging Baltimore Fire in 1904, thus saving the entire section of East Baltimore. That legacy was short lived, however, when citizens in 1911 approved a loan to cover the waterway. The downtown section of the stream located near the shot tower was encased in concrete in 1915.

Stockett wrote that the new roadway covering the stream was "a hideous object, no matter how beneficent it is for trade." The $2 million Fallsway project had the intention of uniting east and west Baltimore, but the wide highway built atop it did just the opposite.

As development expanded the city northward, the Jones Falls was impounded in the 1880s to create Lake Roland in that new city suburb. Other sections were paved over in various projects, such as the construction of Pennsylvania Station in 1911 when the need for parking automobiles took precedence over a picturesque river setting.

In the 1950s, when the automobile began replacing the streetcar as the favored method of commuting, plans were drawn up for the construction of a 9-mile elevated highway to cover

the open stream. It would cost $55 million to build. Baltimore Mayor J. Harold Grady and Governor J. Millard Tawes and other officials cut the ribbon on November 2, 1962.

When finally connected in 1962, the Jones Falls Expressway meant that commuters could leave City Hall and arrive at the beltway just 15 minutes later, more than half the amount of time the trip had taken before. Forty thousand cars would use the JFX every day during its first few years.

By 1977, more than 60,000 cars used the JFX each day, rising to 90,000 in 1985, despite a city that was loosing tens of thousands of residents each and every year. Ironically, today the JFX serves commuters going each direction, as more and more jobs have moved from the city center to the suburbs. The valley today carries an enlarged expressway, the tracks for the Amtrak Northeast Corridor, part of Interstate 83, and the Baltimore Light Rail.

ABOVE *Firefighters were able to keep the Baltimore Fire of 1904 under control around the Jones Falls.*

RIGHT *The downtown portion of the Jones Falls was often filled with pollution due to local heavy industry.*

Steamships DISCONTINUED 1962

While a multitude of steamship companies were based in Baltimore throughout history, perhaps none was better known than the Baltimore Steam Packet Company, referred to locally as the Old Bay Line. It began operations in 1842, and would continue to flourish for the next 122 years. It provided overnight steamboat service primarily between Baltimore and Norfolk, Virginia, among other ports of call in the Chesapeake Bay. The "packet" company name referred to the fact that besides passengers and cargo, the steamships carried mail packets on government mail contracts.

Small, wood burning steamers began plying the Inner Harbor and the Bay as early as the 1820s. The first steamboat to serve Baltimore was the locally built *Chesapeake*, constructed in 1813 to link Baltimore with Philadelphia, Pennsylvania. The Old Bay Line, as it came to be known by the 1860s, introduced what were then massive ships capable of transporting hundreds of passengers long before train travel became the norm. It was noted for its genteel service and fine dining, serving seafood harvested from the Chesapeake Bay.

The company began overnight paddlewheel steamship passenger and freight service daily between Baltimore and Norfolk, under the company's first president, Andrew Fisher Henderson. The route served as a link between the antebellum South and northern markets, hauling large quantities of cotton north and manufactured goods south, along with a thriving passenger business. The company acquired newer and larger ships in the 1850s, such as the *North Carolina* and the *Louisiana*, the latter at 266 feet in length being the largest wooden vessel the company would own. A *Baltimore Patriot* newspaper account in 1852 described the ship's dining saloon as "having imported Belgian carpets, velvet chairs with marble-topped tables, and white paneling with gilded mouldings."

The bridge between north and south was severed during the Civil War years immediately after fighting broke out in April of 1861. The steamship line was unable to serve Norfolk for the duration of the war, going no further south than Old Point Comfort.

By the 1890s, the Old Bay Line had upgraded its fleet with propeller-driven, steel-hulled steamers equipped with modern conveniences such as electric lighting and staterooms with private baths.

The company built a new terminal and headquarters on Light Street in 1898 to accommodate the increasing traffic. Burned and rebuilt following the 1904 fire with a four-sided clock tower, it would remain a local landmark until it was razed in 1950.

World War I doubled freight and passenger business on the line to the busy ports of Norfolk and the Hampton Roads area, with 107,664 passengers using the line in 1917. Catastrophe struck the Old Bay Line on May 24, 1919, when the *Virginia II* caught fire shortly after midnight in the middle of Chesapeake Bay with 156 passengers and a crew of 82 on board. The ship burned completely as many passengers jumped overboard and a lifeboat capsized before being rescued by other boats from the company.

During the Great Depression, the Old Bay Line became one of the first inland steamship companies to promote the carriage of automobiles as a means of filling its ships' empty cargo holds in the 1930s. The Federal government took possession of four of the companies six large ships during World War II, at a time when several steamship companies merged with the Old Bay Line to survive in business. After the war, the line promoted its automobile service to Florida-bound motorists, advertising the elimination of 230 miles of driving by taking the car on an overnight cruise down the Chesapeake to Virginia, while enjoying a sumptuous dinner and relaxing stateroom aboard an Old Bay Line steamer instead of a roadside motel.

One of the Old Bay Line's steamers named *President Warfield* was renamed and became famous as the ship of book and movie fame *Exodus*, when Jewish refugees from war-torn Europe sailed aboard her in 1947 in an unsuccessful attempt to emigrate to Palestine.

By the time the venerable packet line ceased operation in 1962, after 122 years of existence, it was the last surviving overnight steamship passenger service in the United States.

OPPOSITE PAGE *By the time of this 1905 photo, steamer lines were a booming business for Baltimore.*

LEFT *A tug guides the* Arosa Sun *steamship from its stern as the watercraft approach a pier in Baltimore Harbor.*

Streetcars DISCONTINUED 1963

Like many large American cities, streetcars were a popular form of transportation for many Baltimore residents in the late 19th and early 20th centuries. After the Industrial Revolution, residents, who formerly lived within walking distance of their workplace, moved farther away, necessitating a reliable new transportation method to get to and from work, as well as provide transportation for leisure activities and shopping.

In 1859, Baltimore's first horse drawn commuter car began with horses pulling cars on rails. However, with time, cities like Baltimore needed a more reliable and faster method of transport. According to the Maryland State Archives, Baltimore was one of the first cities to experiment with electricity as a power source for its public streetcar transportation; however, attempts to use underground cable were initially unsuccessful, so Richmond, Virginia holds the distinction of the first electric streetcar line, completed in 1888. Richmond's design incorporated overhead wire, which the streetcar connected to via a pole mounted to the roof, a practice that Baltimore would use as well.

The Baltimore Traction Company attempted a cable car system in the early 1890s using stem-driven cables at street level to run cars from Druid Hill Park to Patterson Park; however, its slow moving trains were less favorable to electric streetcars. Baltimore had several different streetcar lines, but in 1899, they merged together into the United Railways & Electric Company.

In addition to the multitude of lines, streetcars also necessitated the erection of power stations and streetcar bars. Additionally, a massive coal power plant was built on Pratt Street between 1900 and 1909. The large brick buildings with multiple smokestacks served as the power source for the United Railways and Electric Company streetcars. It later served as a steam plant for the predecessor of Baltimore Gas and Electric Company and has been readapted as Pratt Street Power Plant, a collection of restaurants and bars.

At its peak, Baltimore had over 400 miles of streetcar lines, with most of the major lines utilizing the old turnpike roads. As Baltimore continued to grow, streetcars not only serviced the downtown core but well into the suburb areas of Reisterstown, Ellicott City, Middle River, Sparrows Point, and Curtis Bay.

After the heyday of the early 1900s, streetcar business began to suffer during the Great Depression. Later, with the advent of the automobile, more and more Baltimoreans preferred to travel by car, and city engineers concluded that streetcars were frankly just getting in the way. Additionally, as more residents moved farther from downtown in newly established suburbs, extending the tracks to reach these people proved to be too expensive. In November 1963, Baltimore's last streetcar went out of service.

With the demise of streetcars, public transportation took the form of city buses and later an underground metro rail. In 1992, the Light Rail, an aboveground rail service, began servicing Baltimore. The 22-mile railway extends from Hunt Valley to downtown Baltimore and farther south to Glen Burnie. Still today, downtown residents use the Light Rail, as do fans attending baseball games at Camden Yards, those needing to go to Baltimore-Washington Thurgood Marshall Airport, and suburbanites in cities such as Timonium and Hunt Valley to commute to downtown Baltimore. A new Red Line is slated to connect Woodlawn to Hopkins-Bayview Hospital campus.

Despite the demise of the streetcars, several monuments still exist, including waiting stations, power stations, and streetcar bars. The Charles Street streetcar barn now houses the popular Charles Theater and Tapas Teatro restaurant. Streetcar lovers can also visit the Baltimore Streetcar Museum near Penn Station.

A campaign by Charles Street Development Corporation and the Charles Street Trolley Corporation, pointing to the success of the new streetcar system in Portland, Oregon, has recently begun with the hopes of bringing back the streetcar to Charles Street. The plan would connect the Inner Harbor with North Baltimore, drawing tourists to the cultural attractions and restaurants of the northern section of the City, as well as providing additional transportation options for residents and college students.

LEFT *As residents moved from the city core, streetcar use increased and families took advantage of them for weekend outings.*

RIGHT *At its peak, Baltimore had over 400 miles of streetcar lines. The cars shown here carried workers from the Bethlehem Fairfield shipyard to downtown Baltimore.*

Old Clubhouse at Pimlico BURNED 1966

Horseracing's Triple Crown is a three-race marathon beginning with the Kentucky Derby in Louisville, Kentucky and finishing with the Belmont Stakes in New York. Sandwiched in between is the Preakness Stakes held the third Saturday in May in Baltimore at the historic Pimlico Race Course. Over 100,000 spectators pack the stands at Pimlico for the Preakness, while much smaller crowds attend the weekday races held there the rest of the horseracing season.

Pimlico Race Course opened on October 25, 1870 by the Maryland Jockey Club. As the second oldest racetrack in the country, racing fans have been fortunate enough to see some of the greatest race horses in Baltimore, including Sea Biscuit, Man O' War, War Admiral, Cigar, and Secretariat. Pimlico was built on 70 acres by the Maryland Jockey Club, which purchased the land for $23,500 and spent $25,000 to build the racetrack. Affectionately called "Old Hilltop" for the spot in the infield that was built up, offering great views (although the hill was removed in 1938), Pimlico Race Course is a historical gem and important sports venue for Baltimore.

When Pimlico opened in 1870, one of the architectural highlights of the new track was the stunning Steamboat Gothic designed Clubhouse (it would later be referred to as the "Old Clubhouse," when a newer one was built in 1960). The elegant, three-story, wooden Clubhouse featured white columns and a massive wraparound porch where spectators could watch horsing legends while feasting on local culinary delights and cocktails. Perhaps its most well known architectural element was the equestrian weather vane on the cupola where the colors of the winning horse were painted to replicate the winner of the Preakness race. This tradition continues today.

The "Old Clubhouse" changed ownership a few times, and was once a high-end social club. Tragically, it was destroyed by an eight-alarm fire just before midnight on June 17, 1966. The cause of the fire was determined to be an electrical malfunction. The new clubhouse, built in 1960, survived. Spectators from the neighborhood raced to Pimlico to watch the fire, and in the early morning hours of June 18, little remained of the grand Old Clubhouse.

ABOVE *An aerial view of Pimlico Race Course showing the clubhouse far left.*

LEFT *The clubhouse's huge wraparound porch gave unparalleled views of the race course.*

OPPOSITE PAGE *The Steamboat Gothic clubhouse (shown far left) was the center of the social scene at Pimlico.*

Bromo-Seltzer Factory RAZED 1969

One of Baltimore's most iconic buildings standing today is the Bromo-Seltzer Tower at West Lombard and South Eutaw Streets. Most tourists take a moment to pose in front of the massive tower and marvel at the four clocks near the top of the building. However, the tower was originally only one component of a much larger structure.

The tower, factory, and administrative office building were all built in 1911 by Captain Isaac Emerson, inventor of Bromo-Seltzer and owner of Emerson Drug Company. Emerson, born in North Carolina in 1859, moved to Baltimore in 1880 after graduating from college as a chemist. He then opened a drug store in Baltimore where he invented a product for headaches and indigestion. He named it Bromo-Seltzer and then formed the Emerson Drug Company. He aggressively

marketed and advertised the patented product globally. Sales were robust, and Emerson made a fortune off Bromo-Seltzer.

In 1911, Emerson took on the ambitious project of building a factory in downtown Baltimore. (Emerson also built the Emerson Hotel, a 17-story hotel, which opened in 1911, closed in 1969, and was demolished in 1971.)

A May 3, 1910 announcement in the *Baltimore Sun* welcomed the new structure to the downtown skyline enthusiastically:

The Bromo-Seltzer tower building will be one of the most novel in the history of local architecture. It will be eight stories high and is to be surmounted by a 200-foot tower, the upper part of which will take the form of a huge bottle. The top of the bottle will be crowned with jeweled lights. The entire structure will be 355 feet tall.

Emerson wanted the tower to be modeled after the Palazzo Vecchio in Florence, reportedly after falling in love with the Palazzo Vecchio on a recent trip. When completed, the tower was the tallest building in Baltimore. Emerson hired well-known Baltimore architect Joseph Evans Sperry for the job. Sperry, born in South Carolina, had moved to Baltimore and formed an architecture firm with James Bosley Noel Wyatt that would last until 1887. After going out on his own, Sperry would design churches, hospitals, banks, and buildings on the campus of Johns Hopkins University. However, his design of the Bromo-Seltzer Tower would be his most famous project.

Originally, the tower featured a 51-foot revolving Bromo-Seltzer bottle on top. The steel bottle was blue and was a large replica of the recognizable blue glass bottles that contained the headache powder. The huge bottle was illuminated and could

be seen up to 20 miles away. In fact, ships approaching the Baltimore harbor would often use the brightly lit bottle as a navigation tool. The bottle, which was 20 feet in diameter, would make two revolutions per minute. However, in 1936, the bottle was removed due to structural concerns and its labor-intensive nature.

In addition to the bottle, the tower's most notable feature is the clock, which still works today. Instead of numbers on the clock face, the letters spelling Bromo-Seltzer are used. There is a clock on each side—four in all—and they were installed by the Seth Thomas Clock Company. The translucent white glass dials are 24 feet in diameter, while the minute hands are 12 feet long. It's the largest four-dial gravity clock in the world.

In 1956, Warner-Lambert Pharmaceutical Company purchased Emerson Drug Company, and in 1967 it moved the production of Bromo-Seltzer to Pennsylvania. In 1969, the City of Baltimore demolished the factory and office building but thankfully saved the tower. In 1973, the tower was placed on National Register of Historic Places and is now utilized as studio space for artists.

OPPOSITE PAGE *The tower was originally topped by a revolving 51-foot replica of a Bromo-Seltzer bottle. A 1947 advertisement for the "fast headache help."*

LEFT *The tower and adjoining Emerson Drug Co. Building.*

RIGHT *Captain Isaac Emerson, inventor of Bromo-Seltzer.*

FOLLOWING PAGES *A panoramic view of Baltimore from atop the tower.*

Original City Baths, Pools and Beaches

WANED 1970s

Today, when Baltimoreans are dirty, they shower. And when they need relief from summer heat, they head to their community pool, country club pool, the pool in their own backyard, or they drive two to three hours to the beach for the weekend. Things were much different on all these fronts in the late 1800s and early 1900s.

In the late 1800s, many Baltimore residents did not have indoor plumbing, and while outhouses provided certain amenities, bathing and showering were not possible. Thanks to the pioneering spirit and diligence of Reverend Thomas Beadenkoff, an 1880 Johns Hopkins University graduate, Baltimore was one of the first major cities to operate a sophisticated system of public bathhouses.

Beadenkoff's first attempt at a public bathhouse was in 1893 in a rudimentary shack that served a certain need, but the reverend envisioned a more widespread system. He was later appointed to the City's Bathing Commission, and he sought funding for a City-operated bath system from philanthropist Henry Walters, who also funded the Walters Art

Gallery in Baltimore. Walters generously paid for the first three bathhouses, and he was present when the first bathhouse opened in 1900 on South High Street in Baltimore's Little Italy neighborhood. Subsequent bathhouses opened on Columbia Street in 1902, followed by another one in 1905 reserved for "coloreds" only. The latter one was rarely used in the beginning, as people were afraid of catching a cold. The baths were a huge success—in 1907, almost 600,000 people utilized them. Eventually, the city would operate six bathhouses and two portable bathhouses that could be moved from street to street. Guests were provided a towel, soap, and a five-minute shower

ABOVE *African-American children use one of the City's temporary outdoor showers.*

LEFT *Residents made the most of Baltimore's public beaches, which included the Maryland Swimming Club.*

RIGHT *Separate baths were built for men and women, while some were built only for "coloreds."*

for five cents. Later, neighborhood schools were utilized as well. The original bathhouse on High Street was torn down in 1954.

The influx of bathhouses led to the creation of public bathing pools in Baltimore. The first one opened in Patterson Park complete with a beach and separate boys and girls areas for bathing. There were also restrictions on when girls and women could swim, and rules on bathing attire for both sexes. The Patterson Park pool remains today. A May 1913 article in the *Baltimore Sun* documented the opening of the season for the public bathing pool, but due to the chilly weather, few showed up. The article also mentioned the pool at Gwynn's Falls, which opened despite not being quite finished (it was later razed). The first pool designated for African-Americans opened in 1921 at Druid Hill Park (there were two pools there). In the Charles Village neighborhood, Lakewood Pool opened in 1921 at 2519 North Charles Street. The semi-private swimming club featured powder-white sand, and bathers included Baltimore natives F. Scott and Zelda Fitzgerald and visiting entertainers appearing at the Hippodrome Theatre, including Milton Berle. Lakewood Pool closed in 1944.

Lack of city funding and waning interest led to the closure of some of the other public pools in Baltimore. Another potential reason was the ongoing controversy over segregation. The pool in Druid Hill Park was the only one designated for African-Americans (they were allowed to use park

facilities at the other public pools but not swim). Later, the NAACP sued and eventually won, forcing the City pools to integrate. In the aftermath, white attendance at most pools plummeted. Fears heightened after a 1962 riot at Riverside Pool when

ABOVE LEFT *Lakewood swimming pool in Charles Village.*
ABOVE *The Gwynn's Falls Swimming Pool was one of Baltimore's many public pools in the 1950s.*

a large group of whites attacked black children in the pool. In 1999, the pool designated for blacks at Druid Hill was filled in after decades of non-use and a memorial dedicated to the segregation fight was erected. The other pool at Druid Hill remains.

In addition to public baths and public bathing pools, Baltimore also once had public beaches. The first one was designed by Reverend Beadenkoff in 1893 at the Canton waterfront area when he got permission from the Canton Company to utilize an abandoned wharf with sheds as a public beach, complete with ropes, floats, and suits. In 1912, the beach had to be abandoned when Standard Oil Company bought the property to build wharves for its boats.

Another public beach was located at Riverview Amusement Park, as well as a very popular South Baltimore beach, Winans Beach. A 1913 *Baltimore Sun* article, however, stipulated that the beach would be closed for the construction of the Western Maryland Railway terminus at Port Covington.

On July 4, 1915, a 500-foot long beach was constructed at historic Fort McHenry. An August 15, 1915 article in the *Baltimore Sun* stated that over 40,000 residents had already enjoyed swimming at the new public beach.

This is the only beach-bathing under the jurisdiction of the Bath Commission and it is well worth a visit to the beach some warm afternoon. Hundreds of visitors line the shore, watching the merry crowd, and all classes and conditions are represented. First, you will see a woman, accompanied by three or four of her children, ranging from seven to 14 years of age, making for their suits. These are largely of the foreign element. Next, you will see a gay party of young men and girls alight from a Carey street car, having come from northern or western sections of the city.

The article also mentioned how people were teaching their children how to swim and how even a crippled man with no legs was enjoying the beach and water. During World War I, the War Department closed the beach, as it took over Fort McHenry.

While a handful of public pools remain, most were gone by the 1970s.

TOP *This 1922 photo shows one of the public baths at School No. 108.*

ABOVE *Public pools offered much-welcomed respite from the oppressive heat of summer.*

LEFT *Philanthropist Henry Walters financed the building of the City's public bath system.*

Waterloo Row RAZED 1970

One of the many victims of "urban renewal" in Baltimore was a stretch of elegant homes called Waterloo Row (named for Napoleon's final defeat at Waterloo in 1815). Built by famed American architect Robert Mills (see sidebar), the 12 homes, located in the 600 block of North Calvert Street, were architecturally known for their thick millwork exteriors and finely detailed interiors.

In 1817, Mills, the president of the Baltimore Water Company, requested that North Calvert Street be graded and paved in anticipation of the construction of Waterloo Row. The area, located north of the city center was undeveloped and considered a risk for speculative housing, especially considering the elegant design envisioned by Mills. In 1819, the 12 homes, which were very wide for row houses, were erected by Mills, along with John Ready, James Hinds, and others. Mills had hoped the homes would attract the attention of the elite residents of Baltimore.

The three-story homes were made of brick and marble with wood interiors and a shingled roof. Other features included dormers, iron railings, marble stoops, elegant mantles, and columns.

OPPOSITE PAGE *The unusually wide rowhouses on North Calvert Street were razed in 1970.*

RIGHT *Robert Mills, who also designed the Washington Monument, erected Waterloo Row in 1819.*

BELOW *The block was documented by a Historic American Buildings Survey.*

Unfortunately, for Mills, the homes were completed during a time of economic turmoil, and the wealthy, elite residents he targeted for sales considered the area too far from the city center and too rural in nature. The homes were valued between $10,000 and $12,000, a high price tag at that time, and for that amount of money, Baltimoreans wanted to live closer to the business district. The fact that the location of Waterloo Row today is in the heart of the cultural district and only a few blocks from the financial district demonstrate how far the city has expanded.

The majority of the homes remained unsold, causing Mills extreme financial hardship. In 1822, Mills had the Baltimore Water Company acquire the homes at a reduced price. Eventually, the homes were razed in 1970. Luckily before this occurred, two first-floor rooms, staircase, furniture, and several interior elements were salvaged by the Baltimore Museum of Art.

In 1991, Waterloo Place apartment buildings, popular with students of the Peabody Conservatory of Johns Hopkins University, was built on the site, allowing the Waterloo name to live on.

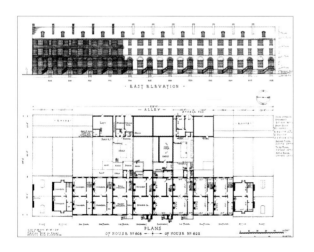

ROBERT MILLS

Robert Mills, the architect of Waterloo Row, was born in South Carolina in 1781. In his early professional life, he had the pleasure of working with some of the most famous architects of the time—James Hoban, Thomas Jefferson, and Benjamin Latrobe, whose influence can be seen in many of Mills's work, especially those dealing with Greek Revival style. After settling in Baltimore, Mills designed St. John Episcopal Church, the Maryland Club, and the Maryland House of Industry. He is known best in Baltimore, however, for his design of Baltimore's Washington Monument (left), which began construction in 1815 and was the first monument built in honor of Washington. The Monument, which still stands today, was located in close proximity to Waterloo Row. Despite the financial setback from the failed Waterloo Row project, Mills's career continued, and his legacy and financial situation seemed secure in 1836 when he beat out competing designs for the Washington Monument to be built in Washington, D.C. In 1848, the cornerstone was laid; however, turmoil with the planning committee, followed by the onset of the Civil War, delayed the construction of the Washington Monument for many years. Mills died in 1855, 30 years before the Washington Monument was completed.

Baltimore Municipal Airport

CLOSED 1960, DEMOLISHED c. 1970

Baltimore-Washington International Thurgood Marshall Airport has become one of the nation's busiest airports. However, until its opening in 1950 as Friendship International Airport, Baltimore was served by a much smaller airport in Dundalk.

Baltimore Municipal Airport (later renamed Harbor Field) was built by the City of Baltimore beginning in 1929. By 1932, the seaplane ramp had been completed and was utilized by Pan American Airlines; however, the use of seaplanes soon fell out of favor. Accommodating land-based aircraft proved to be a more difficult task at Baltimore Municipal Airport. The runways were built on an artificial peninsula along Colgate Creek using silt from the harbor, and construction was delayed for several years, as the silt took longer to dry than expected. Even after the airport finally opened in 1941, the runways buckled under the weight of large aircraft.

Shortly after dedication on November 16, 1941, civilian traffic was suspended in 1942 for use by the United States Air Force for World War II. The airport was used as the headquarters of the 353rd Fighter Group, which also oversaw squadrons in Norfolk, Richmond, and Langley. Additionally, British Prime Minister Winston Churchill flew out of Baltimore Municipal Airport in 1942 on a British Overseas Airways Company flight; the BOA used the airport as its main U.S. Operating Base during the war.

After the end of World War II, the War Department returned control of Baltimore Municipal Airport back to the City of Baltimore and civilian flights returned, servicing over 125,000 passengers a year. That same year, the Maryland National Guard's 104th Fighter Squadron relocated to the airport. Civilian aircrafts flew to such sites as Bermuda and the Caribbean, and traffic steadily increased. With the continuation of the increase of civilian flights, the Maryland National Guard began looking for alternate sites.

The National Guard's need to relocate was eliminated, though, in 1950 when Friendship International Airport opened south of Baltimore in Anne Arundel County. Civilian airlines quickly moved their operations and flights to the newer, more sophisticated airport, leaving more room for the National Guard. In 1950, Baltimore Municipal Airport was renamed Harbor Field.

With the looming conversion to jets, the National Guard realized that Harbor Field's short runways—its longest was 4,520 feet—would not be able to service their needs. In 1957, the National Guard moved to a new facility in Middle River, Maryland. Harbor Field continued to service private planes.

In 1958, the Maryland Port Authority purchased the 356-acre tract called Harbor Field for $4.1 million to construct new port facilities for its ever-expanding maritime business.

Harbor Field was closed on December 30, 1960. The site is now home to the Port of Baltimore's Dundalk Marine Terminal, which is now the Port's largest general cargo facility. The Dundalk Marine Terminal is utilized for the shipment of steel, containers, farm and construction materials. It is also served by Wallenius Wilhelmsen, the largest roll-on, roll-off automobile carrier in the world.

LEFT AND ABOVE *A seaplane lands at Baltimore Municipal Airport. The airport was later renamed Harbor Field.*

RIGHT *The Maryland Air National Guard's 104th Fighter Squadron holds a retreat ceremony in 1947.*

Baltimore Bullets Basketball Team

LEFT TOWN 1973

Baltimoreans are known for their enthusiastic support of local professional and collegiate sports teams. But while fans flock to see the Orioles and Ravens, they do not have the opportunity to support a professional basketball (or hockey) team unless they make the 40-mile drive south to Washington, D.C.

However, from 1963–1973, Baltimore had a National Basketball Association (NBA) professional team, the Baltimore Bullets. The Bullets moved from Chicago to Baltimore in 1963, and just two years later, the team made the playoffs where they upset the St. Louis Hawks before falling to the Los Angeles Lakers in the Western Conference finals. The team continued to flourish, led by stars Earl Monroe and Wes Unseld, and in 1971 the team made its first appearance in the NBA Finals where they were swept by the Milwaukee Bucks.

The Baltimore Bullets continuously made the NBA playoffs, and Baltimore fans were privileged to watch stars such as Gus Johnson and Elvin Hayes. However, in 1973, the Baltimore Bullets moved to Landover, Maryland, just outside of Washington, D.C., and became the Capital Bullets before eventually changing their name to the Washington Bullets. Due to the lack of an adequate arena, the Bullets first played at Cole Field House on the campus of the University of Maryland before settling into the Capital Center in Landover. Despite their move, the Bullets made appearances in Baltimore, as the team played a few games each season in Baltimore in the first few seasons after their move south. Eventually, the Bullets moved to an arena in downtown Washington, D.C.

The Bullets continued their success in the 1970s in their new home, making the NBA Finals in 1975, where they were shocked by Golden State, losing in four games. They regularly made the playoffs, and in 1978, led by Elvin Hayes and Wes Unseld, the Bullets surprised the basketball world by beating the favored Seattle Super Sonics for the NBA title.

In 1995, the Washington Bullets changed their name yet again to the Washington Wizards. Owner Abe Pollin worried that the team's name was too closely associated with violence, which considering Washington, D.C.'s high homicide rate in the 1990s, was not good public relations for the team. Additionally, Pollin was devastated by the assassination of his close friend, Israeli Prime Minister Yitzhak Rabin, and he concluded that "Bullets" was no longer an image he wanted associated with his team. Thousands of new nicknames were suggested for the basketball team, and finally "Wizards" was selected. The name (as well as the cartoonish logo) were criticized, especially by NAACP's Morris Shearin, who complained that the name "Wizards" was associated with the Ku Klux Klan; the KKK's supreme leader is called the Imperial Wizard.

Meanwhile, Baltimore continues to be without a professional basketball team, despite the fact that the nearby University of Maryland basketball team plays before regular sellout crowds. In fact, Baltimore is considered one of the largest metropolitan markets in the United States that does not have a professional basketball or hockey team. The city's proximity to Washington, D.C, and Philadelphia may be in part to blame, but others point to the lack of a modern, adequate indoor sports arena. The 1960s-era 1st Mariner Arena, which holds about 12,000 spectators in downtown Baltimore, plays host to concerts and special events (the Washington Capitals hockey team also recently started holding an annual exhibition game in Baltimore). Many feel that Baltimore has not seriously been considered for an expansion basketball or hockey team, as well as not hosting annual sporting events such as First or Second rounds of the NCAA March Madness basketball tournament, due to its outdated arena.

In 2011, the Greater Baltimore Committee released a plan that calls for a new 18,500-seat arena and hotel—at a price tag of about $500 million—to be built and attached to the Baltimore Convention Center, which would also be expanded as part of the plan at an additional cost of $300–$400 million.

LEFT *Baltimore Bullets center Wes Unseld drives through Los Angeles Lakers defender Wilt Chamberlain and his teammates in this photo from January 1969.*

RIGHT *A publicity shot from November 1954. From left to right: Connie Simmons, Don Hendrickson, Paul Hoffman, Frank Selvy, and Bob Houbregs.*

Fort Holabird CLOSED 1973

Baltimore has a long and storied military past—from the critical defense of Ft. McHenry during the War of 1812 and the penning of the "Star-Spangled Banner" by Francis Scott Key to the first bloodshed of the Civil War during the Pratt Street Riot in 1861. Baltimore was also the site of a large military installation that was especially important during World War II.

Originally called Camp Holabird and established in 1917, the military site was once near Colgate Creek in the Dundalk area in southeastern Baltimore City. Camp Holabird, named after Brigadier General Samuel Beckley Holabird, a Quartermaster General of the United States Army in the late 1800s, the location was chosen not only for its massive undeveloped potential, but also because of its convenient access to rail, water, and road transportation methods. The 96 acres of marshland were used primarily as an Army motor transport training center and depot by the War Department. Other functions included being utilized as a motor transport school, a repair shop for the purpose of assembling vehicles destined for overseas use during World War II, and the crating of the vehicles and shipping them abroad. Camp Holabird was also utilized as a laundry facility for

Camp Holabird, Fort Howard, Curtis Bay, and the Third Corps Headquarters.

In its early stages, Holabird contained more than 21,000 trucks onsite and the "Jeep Willie" was first tested and approved for usage here. The Jeep Willie was a small four-wheel drive utility vehicle that's considered the iconic World War II Jeep and its popular culture influence was furthered by its use in the popular television show, *MASH*.

Its early history also contains a less fortunate chapter—in 1919, a U.S. Navy C-8 blimp exploded during its landing at Camp Holabird en route from Cape May, New Jersey to Washington, D.C., injuring 80 people. Windows in homes a mile away shattered from the explosion's blast.

Camp Holabird began as a site containing a number of canvas tents, but by 1928 it contained nearly 7,000 personnel and approximately $14 million of motor transport stock on hand.

During World War II, Holabird shipped vehicles, parts, and accessories overseas for the war, and was also used as a training facility for the Mid-Atlantic region. After the war, the installation would grow to include approximately 350 acres and 286 buildings. In 1950, Camp Holabird was renamed Fort Holabird and was used as the U. S.

Army Intelligence School and Counter Intelligence Records Facility, as well as an Armed Forces examining and entrance station. In 1971, the U. S. Army Intelligence School and Counter Intelligence Records Facility were closed and moved to Fort Huachuca, Arizona. The Crimes Record Center would later be moved to Fort Belvoir, Virginia.

In the early 1970s, Fort Holabird was used to guard witnesses in major federal cases; Watergate co-conspirators John Dean and Charles Colson were both held at Fort Holabird in a special safe house holding facility.

In 1973, however, Fort Holabird was closed. The City of Baltimore, despite opposition by local citizens in Dundalk, who wanted a recreation space to be created, developed the land into the current Fort Holabird Industrial Park. The former Officers' Club, however, was saved to house Chapter 451 of the Vietnam Veterans of America.

RIGHT *A jeep being tested in 1940. After World War II, Fort Holabird would grow to include approximately 350 acres and 286 buildings.*

BELOW *Originally called Camp Holabird, the fort was named after Brigadier General Samuel Beckley Holabird.*

St. Mary's College and Seminary RAZED 1975

Catholicism has a long and storied history in Baltimore—the Baltimore Basilica is called America's First Cathedral (built between 1806 and 1821) and St. Mary's College and Seminary was the first Roman Catholic Seminary in the United States. In 1791, the Sulpician Fathers, who were well known for their work in France, came to Baltimore at the request of Bishop John Carroll. In what is known today as the Seton Hill neighborhood in West Baltimore, St. Mary's College and Seminary was founded in 1791 on a property called One Mile Tavern. The property served as the home to St. Mary's College and Seminary for 87 years.

Fr. Francis Charles Naget served as the first rector and superior of the Sulpician community. According to the Archdiocese of Baltimore, the Seminary's goal was to produce clergy to assist the newly formed diocese in Baltimore. However, of the five seminarians who began their education at St. Mary's Seminary in 1791, only two were ordained. By 1808, St. Mary's Seminary had a total enrollment of 23 students. In 1822, Pope Pius VII established the seminary as the country's first ecclesiastical (pontifical) faculty with the right to grant degrees in the name of the Holy See. By 1865, the Archdiocese of Baltimore had 18 seminarians in formation at St. Mary's Seminary.

Eventually, additional property was purchased, and the Seminary was centered around Pennsylvania Avenue and Paca Street. Archbishop Bayley laid the cornerstone of the new seminary building on May 31, 1876, and in 1878 a larger building was dedicated, allowing the Seminary to continue to grow.

Sensing the need for further growth, a new location for St. Mary's Seminary was sought out, and an 80-acre lot located near Roland and Belvedere Avenues in the leafy Roland Park area of Baltimore City was purchased. On November 18, 1928, the cornerstone was laid for the new St. Mary's Seminary, and the building was dedicated a year later. The original location was used as the center of philosophy for St. Mary's with the School of Theology moving to the new Roland Park campus. In the 1940s and 1950s, the Seminary had as many as 300 students.

In 1969, seminarians studying philosophy were also moved to St. Charles College, and the Paca Street campus was closed. Five years later, the seminary building and most of the property were sold to the City of Baltimore to develop a park, and St. Mary's Park is now the largest open green space in downtown's West Side. To build the park, the seminary building was razed in 1975.

However, the original seminary chapel, the Mother Seton House, and the former convent, which today houses the St. Mary's Spiritual Center, remain and are known as the St. Mary's Spiritual Center & Historic Site. The chapel, built in 1808, was designed by the renowned French architect Maximilian Godefroy. The Mother Seton House was the home to Elizabeth Ann Bayley Seton, who in 1975 became the first U.S.-born canonized saint within the Catholic Church. The widowed Mother Seton came to St. Mary's in 1808 and lived there with her three daughters until 1809, when she moved to Emmitsburg, Maryland to found a religious congregation and establish a school for girls in Emmitsburg. The Spirituality Center's building was constructed in 1896, and today the Center offers various lectures and programs on the topic of Christian spirituality, as well as individual spiritual direction.

LEFT AND RIGHT *When these 1974 photographs were taken, St. Mary's College and Seminary building was being used as a community learning center.*

Baltimore Colts Football Team LEFT TOWN 1984

Although it's been more than 25 years, the heartbreaking move by the Baltimore Colts to Indianapolis, Indiana in 1984 still pains most Baltimoreans. In addition to being without a football team from 1984 to 1996, the bizarre and abrupt manner in which the team moved deepens the pain.

The Baltimore Colts' history in Baltimore dates back to 1953 when the city was granted a franchise, and in surprising fashion won its first game over the Chicago Bears. Only a few years later, in 1959, the Colts won the Western Division Title and advanced to the NFL Championship game versus the New York Giants in Yankee Stadium, led by Hall of Fame quarterback Johnny Unitas. On December 28, 1958, a national television audience watched what many still regard as the "Greatest Game Ever Played." The first overtime game in NFL history ended when the Colts' Alan Ameche stormed into the end zone for the winning score to give the Colts a 23–17 win. Many credit that game as the catalyst to the rise in popularity for professional football in the United States. The following year, the Baltimore Colts became NFL Champions once again when they defeated the New York Giants for a second time.

The Baltimore Colts were participants in two other memorable NFL championship games. In Super Bowl III, the heavily favored Colts were shocked by the New York Jets, as the Jets' charismatic quarterback, Joe Namath, famously guaranteed a Super Bowl win, a proclamation that seemed ludicrous. Two years later, however, the Colts would win their first Super Bowl with a victory over the Dallas Cowboys.

In 1972, owner Robert Irsay took ownership of the Baltimore Colts, and the following year the franchise's star player Johnny Unitas was traded to San Diego. The team continued to make the playoffs, but by 1978 they began consistently losing and in 1982 attendance at home games began to suffer. The City of Baltimore refused to build a new stadium for Irsay, and in 1983, following a dreadful season, the Colts' Number One draft pick, John Elway, refused to sign with the Colts.

In early 1984, Irsay began talks with other cities, including Phoenix and Indianapolis, about moving the Colts from Baltimore. What's particularly painful for most Baltimoreans is that while Irsay was shopping for a new home for the Colts, he repeatedly claimed publicly that he was not looking to move the team.

Fearing they were on the brink of losing their team, the Maryland legislature intervened, and on March 27, one of its chambers passed legislation giving the city of Baltimore the right to seize ownership of the team by eminent domain. The following day Irsay agreed to a deal with Indianapolis. A fleet of Mayflower trucks was sent to the Colts' Owings Mills, Maryland, training complex after midnight on March 29, 1984, during a snowstorm. Each truck took a different route to Indianapolis, to aid in the team's evacuation under the cover of night. By morning, the team was gone.

A lawsuit between the City of Baltimore and the Irsay family ensued, and ultimately reached the U.S. Supreme Court. In 1985, the lawsuit was thrown out, and in 1986, a settlement was reached between the City of Baltimore and the Colts, where the Colts organization agreed to endorse a new NFL franchise for Baltimore. The Irsay family refused to relinquish the Colts name, records, and history back to Baltimore.

The Irsay family also refused to endorse Baltimore for an NFL expansion franchise, and Baltimore would fail in several attempts at landing a new team, most notably in 1993, when the NFL awarded a team to Jacksonville, Florida. After having a team in the Canadian Football League, the NFL finally returned to Baltimore in 1996 when the Cleveland Browns relocated to Baltimore. The NFL, Cleveland, and Baltimore finally reached an agreement to leave the Browns' name, colors and records in Cleveland, and the Baltimore Ravens were born. In 2001, the Ravens won Super Bowl XXXV, returning the trophy to Baltimore.

LEFT *Baltimore Colts legend Johnny Unitas prepares to pass in a 1967 game.*

RIGHT *Baltimoreans loved their Colts and the city was devastated when the team relocated to Indianapolis.*

Baltimore Shipyards CLOSED 1984

With its proximity to the Chesapeake Bay, Baltimore was a natural location for shipbuilding. A multitude of shipbuilding companies have come and gone throughout the history of the city and the Inner Harbor as technology changed and world wars and other conflicts resulted in massive peaks of production.

Perhaps the best known was the American "clipper ship," which reigned international waters until the advent of steam propulsion. The first Clipper Ship was built in Baltimore about 1815 at the William Skinner shipyard. The firm eventually became the William Skinner & Sons, and would continue until 1899, when it was consolidated as the William Skinner & Sons Shipbuilding and Dry Dock Company of Baltimore City.

With a yard located about a mile below that of William Skinner & Sons, the Columbian Iron Works and Dry Dock Company was also engaged for years in the shipbuilding business. In the early 1890s, the Holland submarine *Plunger* was built there, the forerunner of the naval submarine. In 1896, the commercial submarine known as the *Argonaut* was built at this yard by inventor Simon Lake. At this plant were also built the cruisers *Detroit* and *Montgomery*, the gunboat *Petrel*, the revenue cutter *Seminole*, the torpedo boats *Foote*, *Rodgers*, *Winslow* and *McKee*, and the largest and most palatial ferryboats afloat, the *Robert Garrett* and *Erastus Wiman*.

Kennard's Wharf at the end of Philpot Street later became the site of one of the most successful black-owned businesses in Baltimore, the Chesapeake Marine Railway and Dry Dock Company. Founded in 1866, it employed both black and white workers, serving as a center of the city's shipbuilding industry. Like most yards, it both built new ships and repaired or converted older ones.

It was founded by "highly respected leaders in the social, religious, and political affairs of the black community," including John W. Locks and Isaac Myers. Although its charter included the provision that the company was to exist for 40 years, due to a

LEFT AND RIGHT *The* Liberty *ship shortly after construction at Bethlehem Fairfield shipyards in 1943. The ship weighed 3,200 long tons and was a 10,500-ton cargo vessel.*

misunderstanding, the lease expired in 1884. The company closed that same year.

One shipyard located at the foot of Federal Hill would eventually become the Bethlehem Steel Shipyard. It had previously operated as Skinner & Sons (1827–72), Maister & Reaney (1872–80), Columbian Iron Works & Dry Dock Company (1880–99), Baltimore Shipbuilding & Dry Dock Company (1899–1906), Skinner Shipbuilding & Dry Dock Company (1906–15), and Baltimore Dry Dock and Shipbuilding Company (1915–22)

Baltimore became a major war production center for World War I, and especially World War II. The biggest operations were Bethlehem Steel's Fairfield Yard, on the southeastern edge of the harbor, which built Liberty ships. Its work force peaked at 46,700 in late 1943. Incredibly, by late 1943 nearly 200,000 migrant war workers had arrived from rural southern states of Virginia, North Carolina, West Virginia, Kentucky, South Carolina, and Tennessee.

Baltimore also had drydock companies that lined the Harbor, such as the Maryland Drydock Company, which was started in 1920 as the Globe Shipbuilding and Dry Dock Company of Maryland. The company bought land along the Patapsco across the Bay from Fort McHenry.

Maryland Drydock specialized in ship conversions, upgrades and repairs. During World War II, the company focused on the conversion of numerous warships. Unlike many other shipbuilding companies of the period, it survived the postwar downturn in the shipbuilding industry.

In 1970, the company's yard in Baltimore was purchased by the manufacturer of Fruehauf trailers, which spent $30 million upgrading the site. Unfortunately, adverse economic conditions caused the yard to close in 1984. Bethlehem Steel also closed its massive facility that year, which had grown to take over most of the southeast harbor. Few residents of today's Harborview condominium tower and adjoining rowhouses and marina know that their homes were built on the site of the shipyard.

LEFT *The ship's company on the USS* Baltimore, *c. 1895.*

ABOVE RIGHT *Electric welder Walter Norman (left) was one of the more than 6,000 African-American workers at Bethlehem-Fairfield shipyards. He is seen here with Louis Grisanti on the stern of the SS* Frederick Douglas.

RIGHT *The Columbian Iron Works and Dry Dock Company built the* Plunger *submarine and launched it in 1897.*

The Tower Building RAZED 1986

After the devastating Great Baltimore Fire of 1904, downtown Baltimore was in ruins, except for the few buildings that were fortunate enough to survive the blaze. Shortly thereafter, Baltimore began to slowly reshape its skyline, fueled by a desire to rise from the ashes.

One of the most dramatic buildings to sprout downtown was the Maryland Casualty Building, also called The Tower Building. Located on East Baltimore Street by Guilford Avenue, it was built beginning in 1911 at the site of the former City Hotel.

A *Baltimore Sun* article on April 13, 1911 with the headline, "Tower to Rise 350 Feet" enthusiastically announced the design for the Maryland Casualty Building:

New Maryland Casualty Building Plans Are Out. The structure will include five complete stories and a handsome tower rising 350 feet. The tower will be 47 square feet and contain 11 office floors, with light on all sides. One of the main features of the building will be an immense dial clock at the top of the tower.

A subsequent newspaper article stated that the building's design would be:

a symmetrical tower of artistic design, similar to that of the Metropolitan Tower Building in New York City and the most ornate of its kind south of New York. Surmounting the tower will be installed a powerful beacon light, the rays of which will be discerned all over the city and 20 miles down the bay.

On April 25, 1912, a *Baltimore Sun* article stated that "work on the new home for the Maryland Casualty Company is nearing completion. Most of the exterior work is now finished and the interior is being put into shape. It will be one of the finest office structures in the city." The article stated that Otto Simonson was the architect for the building to be constructed by John Waters at an estimated cost of $300,000.

Upon completion, there was much debate as to whether the new building was now the tallest structure in Baltimore; however, it was determined that the nearby Emerson Tower was indeed tallest with the Maryland Casualty Company building coming a close second.

In addition to its impressive height, the Tower was also notable for its four-sided Seth Thomas clock, which rivaled the iconic Bromo-Seltzer Tower clock in size. The Seth Thomas Clock Company began producing clocks in 1813, and the clock at Grand Central Terminal in New York City was manufactured by the clockmaker. The company also made wall and mantle clocks for residential use until its demise in the 1980s. The clock on the Maryland Casualty Company building was enormous with glass dials measuring 17 feet in diameter with 10-foot hands. When the building opened to the public in 1912, huge crowds came to see not only the clock but also the Observation Tower that offered unparalleled vistas of the city. The building also had an arcade with various businesses, including the Maryland bureau of the Associated Press.

Soon, though, the company outgrew its downtown building, and in 1919 Maryland Casualty relocated to the Roland Park neighborhood in what is now The Rotunda shopping center on 40th Street. At this site, the company also built a clock tower, much smaller in size than the one on East Baltimore Street. The building was converted into a shopping center in 1971.

After Maryland Casualty vacated the downtown tower building, newspaper magnate W.R. Hearst purchased it for $1 million in 1923. He intended to use the building to host his morning and afternoon newspapers, the *American* and the *Baltimore News*. However, Hearst never used the building. In a 1986 newspaper article, former Hearst Corp. employees said, "the California-based publisher feared the constant rumble of printing presses on lower floors of the 18-story building might cause the slender tower to come tumbling down." This same article stated that city engineers deemed the building unsafe in 1986, and it was estimated that $11–12 million would be necessary to renovate it.

In 1942, Hearst sold the building for $500,000 to a Baltimore attorney. Eventually, the building was sold to a partnership headed by developer Bernard Manekin, who bought the building from the Maryland Deposit Insurance Fund for $2.53 million. A demolition permit was sought in 1986, despite the opposition from preservation leaders and an interest by developer Scott Toombs to renovate the building. Manekin did agree to salvage the clock and place it atop an office building planned for the property. However, the office building was never constructed, and the clock was reportedly stored at the Maryland Casualty building on 40th Street.

In 1986, the Tower was demolished, and a parking lot was built in its place.

RIGHT *Upon completion, the Tower was the second tallest building in Baltimore.*

BELOW *William Randolph Hearst bought the Maryland Casualty Building for his local newspapers.*

COPYRIGHTED 1904

McCormick Spice Plant RELOCATED TO THE SUBURBS 1989

Willoughby M. McCormick started his flavoring business in Baltimore in 1889, at the young age of 25. From one room and a small cellar, the initial products were sold door-to-door and included root beer, flavoring extracts, fruit syrups, and juices. The company has since grown into an international behemoth, and 100 years after it was established, it moved its corporate headquarters from Baltimore City to Baltimore County. Its spice processing plant located downtown at 414 Light Street emitted different spice odors depending on what was being manufactured that day.

McCormick began by selling under the "Bee Brand" and "Silver Medal" trademarks. It sold products such as "Iron Glue" (Sticks Everything But the Buyer) and "Uncle Sam's Nerve and Bone Liniment" (For Man Or Beast). Their motto was "Make the Best—Someone Will Buy It."

In 1896, McCormick bought the F.G. Emmett Spice Company and entered the spice industry. Seven years later, Willoughby and his brother Roberdeau incorporated the company in Maine; it was reincorporated in Maryland in 1915. Most of the company's assets and records were destroyed in the Great Baltimore Fire of 1904, although they erected a new five-story building on the same site near the Inner Harbor within 10 months of the disaster.

In 1910 McCormick became one of the first producers of tea in gauze pouches, thereby introducing "tea bags" to the consumer. In 1934, Baltimore architect Edwin Tunis designed and oversaw the installation of an early English Tea House on the seventh floor of the McCormick Building. Friendship Court, a replica of a 16th-century English village, was constructed in the building shortly thereafter. For many years, visitors would take tours of Friendship Court and the Tea House theme was used in packaging and marketing promotions. New metal containers were developed for the spice line, one of the packaging changes that won seven national packaging awards for McCormick in the next several years.

Willoughby's nephew Charles P. McCormick began working for the company in the summer of 1912 and was elected to the Board of Directors in 1925. Willoughby died on November 4, 1932, and Charles was elected President and Chairman of the Board at age 36. In 1938, McCormick's research team developed "McCorization," a spice sterilization process that made McCormick spices the safest and cleanest available with no loss of flavor. The big "Mc" logo became a trademark for nearly all U.S. products in 1941. McCormick acquired A. Shilling & Co of San Francisco in 1947, a coffee, spice and extract house that enabled McCormick to begin countrywide distribution.

The company has since acquired dozens of competing spice companies and flavoring products, including a Baltimore favorite, Old Bay, in 1990. The company moved its headquarters to Sparks, Maryland in 1989, and abandoned its five-story white building situated in the Inner harbor. The building was razed and the site currently serves as a parking lot.

OPPOSITE PAGE *Once located by the Inner Harbor, McCormick relocated in 1989 to Sparks, Maryland.*
BELOW *Tea tasting at the McCormick Building.*

Hutzler's Department Store LIQUIDATED 1990

Hutzler's department store was a fixture in the city's retail trade for over 130 years. It was opened by Abram G. Hutzler in July of 1858. At age 23, Hutzler (1835–1927) was too young to establish his own credit needed to open the store, so his father Moses Hutzler signed the official documents for its creation. It was first known as M. Hutzler & Son, although Moses had nothing to do with running the business. It later changed its name to the Hutzler Brothers Company.

From its beginning as a small dry goods store at the corner of Howard and Clay Streets in Baltimore, Hutzler's eventually grew into a chain of 10 department stores, all located in Maryland.

After Abram brought his two brothers Charles and David into the business in 1867, the retail store was managed by David, while Abram and Charles opened a related wholesale business. The retail store expanded into three other storefronts on Howard Street in 1874, 1881 and 1887, gradually forming into a large department store.

The original Howard Street locations were razed in 1888 and replaced by the five-story Hutzler

Brothers Palace Building designed by Baldwin & Pennington. Over 200 employees worked in several organized departments within the massive building.

Its exterior was composed of Nova Scotia gray stone carved with arabesque heads and foliage, and large display windows. Facing Clay Street, a keystone carved with the image of Moses Hutzler was placed over the main display window.

Hutzler's continued to expand: a five-story building on Saratoga Street and two smaller buildings on Howard Street were added in 1916. In 1924, another five floors were added to the Saratoga Street building, bringing it up to 10 floors. Hutzler's Downstairs, an outlet for discounted merchandise, opened in the store's basement in September 1929.

A five-story, art deco style expansion to the downtown store opened on October 1, 1932. This building eventually extended to nine floors and became known as the Tower building. When it reached the peak of its operations in the 1950s, the downtown location covered an impressive 325,000 square feet of retail space.

In 1952, Hutzler's opened its first branch store in Towson, Maryland, followed by others at Westview Mall, Eastpoint Mall, Harford Mall, and the Inner Harbor area.

In response to declining business in the 1980s, Hutzler's had diminished floor space in its premier location to just 95,000 square feet. The store hired Angelo Arena from Marshall Field's department store in 1983 to attempt to reestablish a successful business model. He relocated the business into a 70,000-square-foot Atrium building next door.

The move to the Atrium was part of a plan to buy four Hochshild Kohn's department store locations and expand Hutzler's from eight to 15 stores in the Baltimore metropolitan area. Arena's efforts were unsuccessful, however, and Hutzler's began closing stores, beginning with the Inner Harbor location in December of 1986.

Descendant David A. Hutzler joined the company's board in 1976 and remained there until 1990, when the company closed and its assets liquidated. Hutzler's remained a family-owned business throughout its 132 years. Its downtown location is believed to be the longest surviving American department store at its original location.

RIGHT *Hutzler's Palace Building had a staff of over 200.*

LEFT *Hutzler's continued to expand their Howard Street store until 1887 when these structures were demolished for a larger building.*

INNOVATIVE RETAILING

According to historian and author Michael J. Lisicky's *Hutzler's: Where Baltimore Shops*, Hutzler's led the retailing industry as one of the first to establish a liberal return policy, granting refunds to dissatisfied customers. It was also the first Maryland retailer with its own fleet of delivery trucks and is believed to be the first chain not to discriminate against African-American customers.

Sun Life Building RAZED 2001

Built in 1916, the Sun Life Building at 109 East Redwood Street (formerly called German Street) was a limestone six-story Beaux Arts building in the heart of downtown Baltimore. The building, the former home of Sun Life Insurance, was made of limestone with tall Corinthian columns. For the most part, the building was in adherence with typical Beaux Arts design features such as formal design, symmetry, and elaborate ornamentation. The Beaux Arts style began to wane in the 1920s, leaving the Sun Life Building as one of the last examples of this French design in downtown Baltimore.

In addition to its beautiful architecture and its contribution as an important element of the streetscape along Redwood Avenue, the building was also historically important to Baltimore, in particular for its Jewish connections. Solomon and Moses Rothschild, who came to Baltimore in 1875 from Bavaria, formed an insurance company in 1890 called the Immediate Sick Benefit Society. In time, this financial company would grow and later become Sun Life Insurance Company of America, one of the largest life insurance companies in the United States.

A Jewish architect was also chosen for the design of the Sun Life Building in Baltimore. Louis Levi, a Baltimore native, was the architect of several synagogues in Baltimore, Philadelphia, and Washington, D.C. Born in Baltimore in 1868, Levi was a Massachusetts Institute of Technology graduate who designed buildings including the Shearith Israel Synagogue in Baltimore and the Sixth and I Synagogue in Washington, D.C., for the Adas Israel congregation. Levi was the first Jewish architect to join the Baltimore Chapter of the American Institute of Architects in 1905.

The Sun Life Building was also the scene of a bizarre rescue shortly after opening in 1916. The January 29, 1917 edition of the *Baltimore Sun* carried the dramatic headline "Locked in Building. Imprisoned Over An Hour, Insurance Man Gets Out by Climbing From Window Ledge." According to the article, G. H. Salter, the Baltimore superintendent, tried to leave for work only to find that his key would not open the front door. After an hour, he started waving his hands and shouting for help. Luckily, a passing patrolman spotted him and devised the escape plan.

Eventually, Sun Life would move to a circa 1966 building at nearby 20 South Charles Street (the building went into foreclosure in 2011), and in 2001 it was reported that the new owner of the East Redwood building had plans to demolish the Beaux Arts building.

Preservationists railed against the measure, citing the historical importance of the building and its architecture. They cited how the Sun Trust Building was once a contributing element in what was called the "Wall Street of the South," a stretch of Redwood Avenue that had a dense concentration of important financial institutions. Preservationists had already lost one battle, as the Sun Life Building's neighbor, the former Merchants' and Miners' Transportation Company building on Light Street (the one referenced in the *Baltimore Sun* article) was razed in September 2000. That building, with its red brick exterior, was one of the first constructed after the fire of 1904.

Originally, the developer said that one of the two buildings—the Sun Life Building or Merchants' and Miners' Transportation Company building—would be saved and incorporated into the design of a new $25 million Residence Inn by Marriott that would be constructed on the site. However, in February 2001, the developers delivered the crushing news that the Sun Life Building would suffer the same fate as its neighbor and be demolished, stating that renovation would be too costly after consulting with architects and engineers. Preservationists, who had battled for more than two years, argued that tax breaks promised by Baltimore City and nonprofits would have helped finance the renovation of the Sun Life Building. However, despite being on the National Register of Historic Places, its designation did not prevent its demolition.

OPPOSITE PAGE *Despite the valiant efforts of preservationists, the Sun Life Building was razed in 2001.*

LEFT AND RIGHT *The Beaux-Arts building was located in the heart of downtown Baltimore.*

Memorial Stadium RAZED 2002

Known as "The Old Gray Lady of 33rd Street" and as "The World's Largest Outdoor Insane Asylum" for its rabid fans, especially during Baltimore Colts games, Memorial Stadium was the former home of Baltimore's baseball team, the Baltimore Orioles, and its NFL team, the Baltimore Colts. In addition, the stadium played host to college football games and even Canadian Football League games.

Situated in northeast Baltimore, Memorial Stadium was built in 1950 at a cost of $6.5 million and included seating for 31,000 spectators. It stood on the grounds of the former Baltimore Stadium built in 1922. Baltimore Stadium played host to college football games and the Baltimore Orioles of the International League beginning in 1944 after the Orioles' Charles Village stadium burned (see sidebar).

Memorial Stadium continued to be the home of the Baltimore Orioles of the International League, and the team enjoyed much success. Then, in 1954, the St. Louis Browns moved to Baltimore, giving the city a major league baseball team. On April 15, 1954, a parade up Charles Street all the way to Memorial Stadium welcomed the Orioles, and Vice President Richard Nixon was on hand for the celebration. Memorial Stadium was also the home to the Baltimore Colts until the team moved to Indianapolis in 1984 and hosted the 1959 NFL Championship game, won by the Colts over the New York Giants.

Memorial Stadium was more than just a place to watch baseball and football. Many of the professional athletes lived in the surrounding neighborhoods, creating an intimacy with the team that fans in most cities today don't experience.

One of the most bizarre incidents occurred on December 19, 1976, when a small private plane crashed into the upper deck of Memorial Stadium on the same day the Colts were hosting the Pittsburgh Steelers in an NFL playoff game. Luckily, there were no serious injuries, as the stadium was rather empty at the time. Unfortunately for Colts fans, the reason there were few fans on hand was because the Steelers were crushing the hometown team, 40–14.

After the Colts' departure from Baltimore, the Orioles continued to play at Memorial Stadium through 1991, when the team moved downtown to the new Oriole Park at Camden Yards. Following

ORIOLE 1921 Base Ball Team.

THE ORIOLES' MANY NESTS

In addition to Memorial Stadium, the Orioles played in several other stadiums during their various incarnations, most of which were in the neighborhood adjacent to Memorial Stadium, Charles Village. The Orioles played in many stadiums in Charles Village, including Oriole Park near 29th Street and Greenmount Avenue in 1889, Union Park at the corner of Barclay Street and 25th Street beginning in 1891, American League Park by Greenmount Avenue, Barclay Street, 28th and 29th Streets, and the second Oriole Park (formerly named Terrapin Park) north of 29th Street from 1914 until July 4, 1944, when the wooden stands burned. The original Oriole Park was only used for two years, as it was considered too far removed from downtown Baltimore. At the second Oriole Park (formerly Terrapin Park) in 1937, a new scoreboard—reported to be 35 feet tall and as wide as four houses—was installed and became known as the largest scoreboard in the world. Its electrical operation was revolutionary for the time, too. During the nighttime fire that broke out in 1944, 1,500 Charles Village residents were forced to flee their homes, and the heat melted asphalt on 29th Street and tar on nearby roofs. Union Park was the site of what was called the "greatest game of the 19th century," when the Orioles played Boston on September 29, 1897. Over 30,000 fans attended, which was the largest crowd ever; however, Boston won, preventing the Orioles from winning their fourth consecutive National League pennant.

the Orioles move downtown, Memorial Stadium was home to the Canadian Football League's Baltimore Stallions, and then in 1996 and 1997 to the Baltimore Ravens, the city's new NFL team. The Ravens played two seasons at Memorial Stadium before moving to a new stadium adjacent to Camden Yards.

After the Ravens left, Memorial Stadium remained empty. The City of Baltimore received many proposals for reuse of the facility; however, it chose to raze the stadium beginning in 2001 through early 2002. Remnants of the stadium were

used to help form an artificial reef in the Chesapeake Bay.

Memorial Stadium's most recognizable architectural element was the enormous plaque that graced the stadium honoring war veterans. On Memorial Day, 2003, an 11-foot-tall, curving black granite wall featuring the well-known phrase from the Memorial Stadium facade ("Time Will Not Dim

RIGHT *Memorial Stadium was once the home to the Baltimore Colts, Orioles, and Ravens.*

the Glory of Their Deeds"), spelled out in the original stainless steel lettering was dedicated at Camden Yards. In another tribute to Memorial Stadium at Camden Yards, an urn containing soil from all foreign American military cemeteries is displayed under glass, and a plaque explains the significance of Memorial Stadium in Baltimore history.

The former site of Memorial Stadium remained vacant until the construction of "Stadium Place," a mixed income housing community for seniors, and the Harry & Jeanette Weinberg Family Center Y. Also, a new recreational sports field was constructed on site.

OPPOSITE PAGE *Located in the Waverly neighborhood, fans would often walk to Orioles and Colts games.*

LEFT *The large plaque honoring veterans was an iconic element of the stadium.*

ABOVE *After the departure of the Ravens, Memorial Stadium stood empty for many years.*

Manufacturing in Canton ENDED 2005

Canton has changed dramatically over the past 200 years. What was once a very industrial neighborhood—dominated by factories, distilleries, breweries, and mills—is now a residential neighborhood full of high-end homes, restaurants, and quaint watering holes.

Canton was founded by Captain John O'Donnell, who was born in 1749 in Baltimore. Later he worked at the East Indian Company, and in the 1780s he began shipping goods from Canton, China. He named his plantation, the home to modern-day Canton, after the Chinese port. The development of Canton was jump started by the formation of the Canton Company, a real estate development firm, in 1829. By the mid-19th century, the once undeveloped neighborhood was home to a cotton mill, furnaces, steel mills, shipyards, brickyards, a distillery, among other industries. One of the industries that had the greatest impact on Canton was the Baltimore Copper Smelting Company, which, like many other companies, relied on an immigrant workforce, most notably Welsh immigrants who lived in the neighborhood in homes built by the company. Canton was also a popular settling place for Irish, German and Polish immigrants. The Canton Company also formed its own railroad in the 1870s,

the Union Railroad, which helped spur growth in the neighborhood.

Due to its waterfront location, Canton was home to shipyards as well as several oil refineries. According to Norman G. Rukert in his book, *Historic Canton*, in the 1860s and 1870s, Canton was believed by many to be the industrial center of Baltimore, and the Canton Oil Works Company was formed by Thomas Poultney, J.M. Moale, Joseph Merritt and Samuel Merritt. Several other refineries were formed, and in 1877 they were consolidated to form the Baltimore United Oil Company, which would later be sold to Standard Oil. Like its neighbor across the water, Federal Hill, Canton also had several fertilizer companies.

The history of Canton's American Can Company goes back to the early 1900s. In 1869, Edwin Norton, a tinsmith by trade, and his brother organized the Norton Brothers Co. of Chicago to manufacture tea and coffee canisters, and the later named Norton Tin Can & Plate Company opened a manufacturing plant in Canton called the American Can Company. In 1908, the American Can Company became the world's largest can-making company when it purchased the Sanitary Can Company of New York. The Canton plant was particularly successful for the company due to the availability of tin plate at Bethlehem Steel and

proximity to shipping and railroad transportation lines. The factory closed in the late 1980s, and the property was vacant for many years. In 1994, more than half of the property was sold to the Safeway grocery store chain, which demolished most of the existing buildings. Three years later, The Can Company LLC acquired the remaining 4.3 acres and 300,000 square feet of remaining historic buildings and redeveloped them into a shopping and retail complex that still stands today.

Around the same time as the heyday of the American Can Company, one of Canton's other thriving businesses was formed, the Potomac Poultry Food Company, which began operations in 1911, according to Rukert. The company crushed oyster shells for poultry feed and lime for fertilizer.

As with many neighborhoods in Baltimore, Canton was heavily influenced by railroad, most notably the 1917 erection of the Pennsylvania Railroad Canton Coal Pier to carry coal from railroad cars out to the pier, helping make Baltimore the East Coast's top coaling port.

Canton was home to several other industrial plants, including the massive Broening Highway General Motors Plant, which opened in 1935 to produce Chevrolets. By 1979, the plant site had increased to more than 160 acres and employed 7,000 employees. The plant closed in 2005.

LEFT *In the early 1900s, the American Can Company was the largest can-making company in the world.*

RIGHT *Canton was home to cotton mills, oil refineries and steel mills.*

BELOW *Canton was heavily influenced by the thriving railroad system.*

Rochambeau Apartments RAZED 2006

The reasons for the razing of a historic building are endless—dilapidated state, structural issues beyond control, urban growth, the need for more housing or office space, and so on. One of the more peculiar reasons came via the 2006 demolition of the historic 101-year-old Rochambeau Apartment building in the Mt. Vernon area of midtown Baltimore City.

Built in 1905 at the corner of Charles and Franklin Streets, the Rochambeau Apartment Building was named for the French commander who camped on the apartment building's site during the Revolutionary War. The seven-story Renaissance Revival building was designed by noted architect Edward Glidden, who also designed the Washington Apartments on Charles Street in Mount Vernon, Archbishop Curley High School, the Furness House, and many other buildings in Baltimore. In addition to its noted architect and 100-plus-year age, the building was iconic in its architecture for its dormer style front

and was an important building in the Cathedral Hill National Register Historic District.

The Rochambeau was also valued by preservationists and historians in Baltimore as it was constructed shortly after the Great Baltimore Fire of 1904, and the Cathedral Hill district played an important part in the city's revival. The area was described in a national register description in this way: "An almost continuous line of stone and brick facades on Charles Street which led to its being described as the 'Rue de la Paix' or 'Fifth Avenue' of Baltimore."

The Rochambeau Apartment building may have been admired by many; however, it had one really big thing going against it—it stood in the shadow of the Basilica of the National Shrine of the Assumption of the Blessed Virgin Mary, also known as the Basilica. Designed by Benjamin Henry Latrobe, who also designed the U.S. Capitol in Washington, the Basilica is called America's First Cathedral (built between 1806 and 1821), and in addition to serving as a place of worship, the Basilica is also a huge tourist draw for visiting Catholics. In 2002, the Archdiocese of Baltimore paid $3.5 million for the Rochambeau. Although the Basilica initially reassured preservationists that they had no plans to raze the apartment building, later, as part of a $30-million-plus renovation plan, it revealed that the Rochambeau was beyond restoration. More important, the historic apartment building blocked visitors' view of the iconic Basilica from Charles Street, the main thoroughfare of the neighborhood. The Basilica wanted to create more of a campus feel around the religious site, and embarked on plans to demolish the Rochambeau to build a prayer garden in honor of Pope John Paul II.

Preservation groups fought the decision, but to no avail. The City of Baltimore even considered giving the Archdiocese a $900,000 subsidy to allow for the church to renovate the Rochambeau and convert it to condominiums as the neighborhood had seen a spike in the development of new condos. The Archdiocese was not interested, however, and when Baltimore Housing Commissioner Paul T. Graziano approved the church's demolition application, the Rochambeau's fate was sealed, and it was razed in 2006.

ABOVE *The Archdiocese razed the Rochambeau in 2006.*

LEFT *The building was named after a French commander, Jean-Baptiste Donatien de Vimeur, Comte de Rochambeau.*

RIGHT *The seven-story Renaissance Revival building was designed by noted architect Edward Glidden.*

RIGHT *For more than 50 years, a mysterious guest would leave offerings on Poe's grave to mark the poet's birthday.*

The Poe Toaster CEASED 2009

Many cities claim the acclaimed poet Edgar Allan Poe as their own. Boston claims him as he was born there, while Richmond, Virginia points out that he spent a great deal of his childhood there. Philadelphia and New York City make the claim based on the fact that he wrote some of his greatest works in those two cities. Poe lived in many cities, but it was in Baltimore in 1849, that Poe died. Because he is buried in Baltimore, residents lay claim to the early master of the horror story and the founder of detective fiction. In 1996, when the National Football League returned to Baltimore, a fan contest to choose the mascot name for the new team was held, and the mascot "Ravens" was selected in homage to Poe's most famous poem, "The Raven."

Poe, born in 1809, had an aunt who lived in Baltimore, and he would later marry his cousin, Virginia Eliza Clemm, in 1835. His death in 1849 was mysterious—just like most of his writing—as he was found wandering the streets in someone else's clothing before his still-unexplained death on the streets of Baltimore. He was buried with an unmarked grave until a monument with a relief bust of Poe, designed by George A. Frederick, architect for City Hall in Baltimore, was dedicated in 1875. According to the Edgar Allan Poe Society of Baltimore, among those in attendance for the dedication was Walt Whitman.

The small cemetery at Westminster Hall, located near the University of Maryland, Baltimore campus, is a frequent tourist spot today, but for more than 50 years, one night in particular was chosen by Poe fans to honor their literary hero. Each year on January 18, Baltimore residents, as well as tourists from around the country, would gather in the late night hours outside Poe's grave waiting for the stroke of midnight and the onset of January 19 to honor the anniversary of Poe's birthday.

However, those gathered, braving many times frigid temperatures, were there for another reason—to catch a glimpse of the mysterious "Poe Toaster," an unnamed person who would slip through the shadows and leave a half-emptied bottle of cognac and three red roses on Poe's grave, a tribute to the beloved literary hero. There's debate as to when the tradition began but most agree that the so-called Poe Toaster began visiting Poe's grave in 1949, the 100-year anniversary of his birth, and a newspaper article in 1950 mentions the mysterious visitor. The significance of the cognac is also debated, while most agree that the three roses are for the three persons buried there—Poe, his wife, and his mother-in-law.

There's been much speculation, as well, as to the identity of the "toaster." Some have claimed to be the person in question, however, their stories have not matched up with historical facts. Many have suspected Jeff Jerome, former curator of the Edgar Allan Poe House and Museum in Baltimore; however, Jerome has always denied such claim. For 15 years, Jerome spent the night inside the former church near the grave with friends awaiting the arrival of the "Poe Toaster," while keeping an eye on the revelers gathered outside Poe's grave.

According to the Edgar Allan Poe Society of Baltimore, in 1993, a note was left for Jerome stating that "the torch will be passed," and another note left in 1999 indicated that the original "Poe Toaster" had died within a few months before the annual event. After 1993, sightings of the visitor suggested two younger persons were exchanging the obligation between themselves, presumably in honor of their father. The annual visitations continued through 2009, the bicentennial of Poe's birth, and after three years of no-show by the "Poe Toaster," on January 19, 2012, Jerome officially declared that the original tradition had ended, bringing an end to one of Baltimore's most beloved and quirky traditions.

LEFT *Edgar Allan Poe is buried at Westminster Hall.*

RIGHT *Despite the absence of the "Poe Toaster," fans can still visit the Poe House and Museum at 203 Amity Street.*

Bethlehem Steel Plant at Sparrows Point

CLOSED 2012

Sparrows Point is an unincorporated area in Baltimore County, Maryland, adjacent to Baltimore and Dundalk, Maryland. The point is named for early landowner Thomas Sparrow, who was granted the land in 1652 by Cecilius Calvert, the 2nd Baron Baltimore. His son Solomon Sparrow established an estate on the property called "Sparrows Nest."

Sparrows Point remained largely rural until 1887, when an engineer named Frederick Wood realized that the marshy inlet would make an excellent deep-water port for the Pennsylvania Steel Company.

Steel was first made at Sparrows Point just two years later by the company, beginning in 1889. By the mid-20th century, Sparrows Point was the world's largest steel mill, stretching four miles wide and employing tens of thousands of workers. It used the traditional open-hearth steelmaking method to produce ingots, both a labor and energy intensive process.

Purchased by Bethlehem Steel in 1916, the mill's steel ended up as girders in the Golden Gate Bridge in San Francisco and in cables for the George Washington Bridge in New York. The plant was a vital part of war production during both World War I and World War II. Bethlehem also purchased the Sparrows Point Shipyard site in 1917, which had been established in 1889 by the Maryland Steel Company. It was a major center for shipbuilding and ship repair and delivered its first ship in 1891.

During the mid-20th century, the shipyard, known as "BethShip," was one of the most active in the United States, delivering 116 ships in the seven-year period between 1939 and 1946.

By 1961, the mill was producing 672,000 tons of steel per year. But changes in the steel industry, including a rise in imports and a move toward the use of simpler oxygen furnaces and the recycling of scrap, led to a decline in the use of the Sparrows Point complex during the 1970s and 1980s. Bethlehem Steel did invest millions in upgrades and improvements to the shipyard, however, making it one of the most modern shipbuilding facilities in the country. This included the construction of a large graving to allow for the construction of large supertankers up to 1,200 feet in length and 265,000 gross tons in size.

From 1984 through 1986, an effort to modernize resulted in additional production, but the success was short lived. Bethlehem Steel went from one financial crisis to another throughout the 1980s and 1990s, selling the shipyard to Baltimore Marine Industries Inc., in 1997 as part of an unsuccessful restructuring attempt. Baltimore Marine operated the facility as a ship repair and refurbishment yard until 2003, when Baltimore Marine Industries collapsed in bankruptcy.

The shipyard complex was sold at auction to Barletta Industries Inc. in 2004. Barletta attempted a redevelopment of the site for use as a business and technology park, and planned to revive shipbuilding on at least part of the site, making use of the modern graving dock added in the 1970s.

The steel plant itself was owned by Mittal Steel following its acquisition of Bethlehem Steel successor International Steel Group in 2005. In 2006 and 2007, a controversial lawsuit by the U.S. Department of Justice directed Mittal to sell Sparrows Point to avoid a monopoly of tin-plated steel. In March 2008, the plant was sold to the Russian company Severstal for $810 million.

The mill was subjected to decreasing

OPPOSITE PAGE *The massive complex was home to over 9,000 people in the 1920s.*

LEFT *Sparrows Point ship construction workers.*

COMPANY TOWN

Like many large manufacturing companies, Bethlehem Steel built a company town adjacent to the Sparrows Point steel complex. The town of Sparrows Point was built beginning in the 1890s, and quickly grew to include thousands of homes, six churches, restaurants, businesses, and banks. It was home to more than 9,000 people in the 1920s, who were attracted to the cheap rent offered by the company—about $35 a month for a six-room house. The entire town is now lost, however, as it was incrementally razed in several stages over several decades in the 1940s to the 1970s to make way for a multitude of Bethlehem Steel plant expansions.

production and layoffs, caught up in the global steel decline, as well as financial problems that Severstal encountered in Russia. In March, 2011, RG Steel, a division of the Renco Group bought the mill from Severstal. A little more than a year later, it filed for bankruptcy and effectively closed the mill.

In August, 2012 a bankruptcy judge in Delaware approved the sale and liquidation of Sparrows Point to Hilco Trading and Environmental Liability Transfer for the incredibly low bid of $72 million. The new owner immediately laid off the 1,975 steelworkers, closed the plant, and began to dissemble and sell its components in the fall of 2012.

Arabbers WANED MID-1960s TO PRESENT

"Holler, holler, holler, till my throat get sore. If it wasn't for the pretty girls, I wouldn't have to holler no more. I say, Watermelon! Watermelon! Got 'em red to the rind, lady!"

These words, sung by Earl Dorsey, a well-known Baltimore arabber, are just some of the folksy, whimsical songs sung by African-American men called arabbers, or hucksters—men who sell fresh produce from horse-drawn wagons in Baltimore City. Arabbers used to be popular in large cities on the East Coast, most notably Philadelphia, Baltimore, and New York City; however, only in Baltimore do arabbers remain, although their numbers are dwindling for many reasons, including diminishing profits, outcry from animal rights advocates, and battles with Baltimore City government over a host of issues.

The term "arabber" means people who "arab," or sell food from horse-drawn wagons, and arabbers have been a mainstay in Baltimore since the 19th century. The arabber harkens back to a time when all goods were sold and delivered via horse-drawn wagon—ice, milk, food, and other household goods. Since World War II, arabbers in Baltimore have been primarily African-American men who distinguish themselves by creating lyrical songs to sell their goods, while entertaining neighborhoods. Recognizable by the brightly colored red and yellow wagons and horses sporting "Baltimore harnesses," complete with white plastic rings and red tassels, arabbers also gain attention by bells on the wagons that let residents know they are approaching. Arabbers are also many times a family affair, most notably the Savoy family led by Donald Savoy who has been an arabber for over 50 years.

Arabbers are also known for packing their wagons full of fresh produce; oftentimes, it appears as though the watermelons, strawberries, bananas, and other fruit will tumble onto the ground, but somehow they stay on the wagons. Arabbers have always played a pivotal role in urban areas of Baltimore—neighborhoods known as "food deserts," due to their lack of grocery stores and other access points for fresh fruits and vegetables.

The decline of arabbers in Baltimore dates back to the mid-1960s when Baltimore City began placing restrictions on new horse stables being constructed, while allowing those already in existence to be grandfathered in. Another big blow to the arabbers was when the large wholesale produce market that had been located in the Inner Harbor area for over 200 years was relocated to Jessup, 15 miles from Baltimore, making it more difficult for many arabbers to purchase produce at a low enough price point in order to resell it and still make a profit.

Other challenges include outcry from animal welfare advocates, who have criticized the living and working conditions of the horses, as well as the Baltimore City government. In 1994, the Arabber Preservation Society, led by Daniel Van Allen, was created to help support and preserve the arabbers, recognizing their important role as an "African-American folk tradition and economically viable system and a method of apprenticeship completely unique to Baltimore," according to the non-profit organization, which adds to its mission to help arabbers "continue their vital and autonomous economy without interfering with their self sufficiency and tradition."

The Arabber Preservation Society was formed after the stables on Retreat Street in Baltimore, one of the few remaining, were condemned due to building code violations and the arabbers and their horses were forced to vacate. Volunteers helped with repairs and to help negotiate with Baltimore City. In 2008, the Retreat Street stables were razed. The horses, who had been moved to Bowie, Maryland, and then to Pimlico Race Course, were eventually relocated to a temporary home—a tent stable in Southwest Baltimore after the City had announced that there was inadequate funding to build a permanent new stable. The temporary tent stables were removed in 2009, and the horses were again removed, sparking a "Day of Outrage" demonstration at City Hall in support of the arabbers. The horses were later returned, and the Arabber Preservation Society, with assistance from Preservation Maryland and Baltimore City Heritage Area, restored the stable on Carlton Street in the Mount Clare neighborhood, as well as the wagons used by arabbers.

What was once a commonplace fixture, especially around Hollins Market in southwest Baltimore, is now, according to the Arabber Preservation Society, down to three horse-drawn wagons in the whole of Baltimore.

RIGHT *Arabbers sport brightly colored wagons to draw customers' attention.*

BELOW LEFT AND RIGHT *Lower-income neighborhoods especially benefitted from the presence of arabbers, but the condemnation of their horses' stables helped lead to their demise.*

INDEX

OTHER TITLES IN THE SERIES

ISBN 9781862059344

ISBN 9781862059924

ISBN 9781862059931

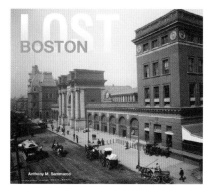

ISBN 9781909815049

ISBN 9781909815032

ISBN 9781909108448

ISBN 9781909108714

ISBN 9781909108639

ISBN 9781862059351